Perfect Balance

Perfect Balance Create time & space for all parts of your life

Paul Wilson

JEREMY P. TARCHER/PENGUIN

a member of Penguin Group (USA) Inc.

New York

JEREMY P. TARCHER/PENGUIN
Published by the Penguin Group
Penguin Group (USA) Inc., 375 Hudson Street, New York, New York 10014, USA * Penguin Group
(Canada), 90 Eglinton Avenue East, Suite 700, Toronto, Ontario M4P 2Y3, Canada (a division
of Pearson Penguin Canada Inc.) * Penguin Books Ltd, 80 Strand, London WC2R 0RL, England *
Penguin Ireland, 25 St Stephen's Green, Dublin 2, Ireland (a division of Penguin Books Ltd) *
Penguin Group (Australia), 250 Camberwell Road, Camberwell, Victoria 3124, Australia (a division of
Pearson Australia Group Pty Ltd) * Penguin Books India Pvt Ltd, 11 Community Centre, Panchsheel
Park, New Delhi – 110 017, India * Penguin Group (NZ), 67 Apollo Drive, Mairangi Bay, Auckland 1311,
New Zealand (a division of Pearson New Zealand Ltd) * Penguin Books (South Africa) (Pty) Ltd,
24 Sturdee Avenue, Rosebank, Johannesburg 2196, South Africa

Penguin Books Ltd, Registered Offices: 80 Strand, London WC2R 0RL, England

First published in 2005 by Penguin Group (Australia)
First Jeremy P. Tarcher/Penguin edition 2007

Most Tarcher/Penguin books are available at special quantity discounts for bulk purchase for sales promo-
tions, premiums, fund-raising, and educational needs. Special books or book excerpts also can be created
to fit specific needs. For details, write Penguin Group (USA) Inc. Special Markets, 375 Hudson Street,
New York, NY 10014.

Library of Congress Cataloging-in-Publication Data
Wilson, Paul, date.
Perfect balance: create time & space for all parts of your life / Paul Wilson.
—1st Jeremy P. Tarcher/Penguin ed.
p.   cm.
"First published in 2005 by Penguin Group (Australia)."
ISBN 978-1-58542-562-4
1. Time management.   2. Self-management (Psychology).   3. Conduct of life.   I. Title.
BF637.T5W55   2007   2006101468
158—dc22

Printed in the United States of America
1   3   5   7   9   10   8   6   4   2

Book design by John Canty © Penguin Group (Australia)

While the author has made every effort to provide accurate telephone numbers and Internet addresses at
the time of publication, neither the publisher nor the author assumes any responsibility for errors, or for
changes that occur after publication. Further, the publisher does not have any control over and does not
assume any responsibility for author or third-party websites or their content.

Neither the publisher nor the author is engaged in rendering professional advice or services to the
individual reader. The ideas, procedures, and suggestions contained in this book are not intended as a
substitute for consulting with your physician. All matters regarding your health require medical supervi-
sion. Neither the author nor the publisher shall be liable or responsible for any loss or damage allegedly
arising from any information or suggestion in this book.

Contents

THE LIFE PRIORITIES CALCULATOR

When will it be perfect?

Won't life be perfect when . . .

- you feel you have all the time in the world—for your family and friends, for your own needs and development?
- you can accomplish more without working harder or longer?
- you're motivated and inspired?
- you perform at your best—unhurried, unpressured, and calm?
- you make sound decisions and quickly recover from setbacks?
- your world is simple and uncluttered?
- life has meaning and purpose, and you're making a difference?
- you discover real peace and contentment?

There's no rush. You don't have to read this book in one continuous sitting. If you find the answer you're looking for in the first few chapters, you don't even have to read the rest.

If it takes you nine months to get to the part that changes your life, so what? You'll have enjoyed every step along the way.

So relax and take all the time you need. When you come to the parts that please you, draw them out. Ease your way through them at your leisure.

If you come to parts that make you feel uncomfortable, put them aside for a while. This is meant to be a relaxing experience— as far removed from work as you can imagine.

Are you expecting this to be a book about work-life balance? After all, that's what everyone seems to be talking about today. If so, you'll find everything you're looking for here.

Then you're going to find more. Much more.

You're going to discover there's more to perfect balance than work—even if it is the most pressing area for most of us. You're going to discover that all the other parts of your life can be enriched at the same time as you put work into a more satisfying perspective.

So, while we'll certainly be addressing the work issue, something far more rewarding awaits: a powerful, life-restoring change that will have you looking back on this moment with fondness and wonder.

This is what perfect balance is about.

It's not just about work

There are those who believe work-life balance to be the most pressing industrial issue of the modern age; certainly it's one that almost every worker, parent, child, friend, and partner has to face up to at some stage.

You may wonder: What is the ideal balance between your primary work on the one hand, and your needs, responsibilities, and aspirations on the other? What is the ideal balance between career and family? Between playmate and provider? Between work and pleasure? Between home life and social life? Between personal growth and professional growth?

Why do some people seem to take it all in their stride, while others feel they have to slog it out, feeling more and more trapped and unsatisfied?

If the only issues at stake here were work life and home life, then it simply becomes a matter of reorganization of activities. You don't need this book in order to achieve that. But while such a move would produce a kind of balance, it's far from perfect balance.

Balance can mean vastly different things to different people. In some quarters, it's seen as an industrial issue to be resolved with more flexible arrangements and benefits. Suggestions include staggered or annualized work hours, shift-swapping, job-sharing, childcare, training, tele-working and self-rostering. Many enlightened employers are beginning to discover that this can deliver a real bottom-line advantage.

The individual's perception of balance can vary even more.

- The senior executive's version may involve having a few more hours each week to spend with family.
- The solo parent's version may involve access to additional childcare, or a few spare hours each week for his or her social life.

- The mature employee's version may involve job security or job-sharing.
- The unemployed person's version may involve having something meaningful to do between 9 and 5.
- The trainee's version may involve more time for education.
- The spiritually oriented person's version may involve finding space for meditation each day.
- The lonely person's version may involve developing occasional social contacts outside work.

In researching this book, we interviewed people from all walks of life to see how their perceptions of "balance" compared. Just as each person was different, their perception differed as well. Even more confusing, it varied according to what was going on in their life at that time.

Fortunately, it takes no more effort to bring multiple perceptions into line than just one of them. So our focus will be on bringing balance to all aspects of your life.

Everything is just perfect

This feeling—of everything being just right and making sense, when you perform at your best and most productive without stress or distraction, when you are motivated and inspired, when you can relax and enjoy the company of others, when you have all the time in the world—is achievable.

This is what we call perfect balance.

Let's see if you can remember experiencing a moment like this. . . .

For a moment, everything around you seems just right. Not an instant of ecstasy or brilliance, but something more subtle. When everything seems to make sense and fall into place. This is not a feeling you analyze in any way; it's just something you're aware of. You feel content and unhurried, with not a worry in the world. You feel accepted, loved, and respected. Whatever you're doing—working, playing, cycling, skiing, painting, nursing, conversing—you're doing smoothly and effortlessly. For the sheer joy of doing it, without thinking about or being conscious of details or outcomes. There is no one particular aspect of this feeling that stands out—it all just makes sense. Your life feels complete.

Have you ever felt something like that?

When the many competing aspects of your life are in balance, this is the kind of feeling you enjoy.

For most people, it's a rare occurrence. Sometimes you get a small taste of it on vacation, or when a problem is solved, or in the early stages of a new relationship, or when something you have been struggling with just "clicks." Mostly, though, it's a fleeting experience, and not something you normally associate with everyday living.

But if you can attain it, and sustain it, it can be the difference between feeling unsatisfied and restless, or feeling happy, content, and whole.

By the end of this book you will have the techniques and strategies required to accomplish this.

The Calm Way: Perfect balance is always closer than you think.
Yet most people are looking for it far away.

Equilibrium restored

Now, let's see if you can remember experiencing something like this. . . .

Your life is in order. If anyone were to ask, you'd say it felt reasonably well balanced. There are occasional ups and downs, and like most people, you get a bit stressed and angry from time to time. But mostly you feel pretty much in control, and everything seems in place.

Then out of the blue, disaster strikes. Your plans are in tatters, you are hit by a setback worse than you ever considered, and your world is turned upside down.

What do you do?

Many people crumble at this point, despairing at how to recover and thinking that their lives may never be the same again. Yet others intuitively know the next step to take, and even though they feel a bit numbed by the experience, they instinctively follow the course that will restore the balance to their life.

This ability to move on, to quickly recover from setbacks, to effortlessly restore the balance, is achievable. Isn't that what you'd expect from perfect balance?

Work and play in perspective

See if you remember this feeling . . .

You go to work in the morning, enjoy what you do during the day, and feel you've accomplished something when your workday comes to an end. When you arrive home, you're immediately in an energetic "home" frame of mind. Work never enters your thoughts. You spend a rewarding evening with your family or friends, or a favorite pastime. Then, when it's time for bed, you feel fulfilled, satisfied, and that life is all right.

As ordinary as it appears, the simple, unpressured nature of this experience is something many people ache for. Especially those who feel so pushed and pressured by their work that they sometimes think of home and nonoccupational parts of their lives as extra obligations, as even more that they have to squeeze into their schedule.

Yet, there were times when it was not like this. There were times when you felt fulfilled, enriched, and entertained. When all the little jigsaw pieces of your life fell into place, and your everyday existence was in balance.

This ability to live a complete life—where you have fun and feel useful, and where work, home, friends, and your other interests all seem to dovetail seamlessly—is achievable. This is what we call perfect balance.

The discovery behind perfect balance

In 1994 one of my researchers came to me with an insight. We'd been exploring the relationship between measured states of inner calm and high levels of achievement. Our models were a variety of successful, accomplished, creative, or outstanding people in many different fields. We used a variety of technologies to evaluate the physiological and mental approaches they used when performing at their peak.

My researcher's observation was that when a certain state was adopted, the most outstanding results came—not by increasing effort but by *reducing* it. You could actually achieve more by striving less.

Yes, by taking it easy.

The Calm Way: The easier you approach it, the better you perform.

We have long known that such an approach was the key to success in sport, the arts, and healing, but the possibility that it could be applied to other aspects of life was seductive.

Imagine being able to convince your boss that going home early today is a sure way to produce a superior result in your work. Imagine that when times get tough, instead of having to employ more effort to achieve what you want, you use less.

Imagine being able to restore the balance in your life—getting the mix right between work and play, improving your family relationships without compromising your career goals, and finding the time to take care of your own needs—with even less conscious effort that you're making now.

When you can do this, you'll know what perfect balance is like. You *can* do this.

You can try the hard way . . .

The approach most people take to any life or work issue is predictable: they slog it out. They force themselves to concentrate. They lather the task with logic and practicality. They apply all the intelligence or physical effort they can muster. And, ideally, they edge ahead in steady, incremental steps.

That's the hard way.

Conventional wisdom says that this is the way to go. From the earliest years, we've been conditioned to believe that exertion achieves all. Our parents, teachers, and advisers insist that anything worth having is worth struggling for, and that success comes to those who work long and hard at it. Our experience in the physical world confirms this: we discover that when we lift, squeeze, or push, the more effort we apply, the greater the result. So we take the same approach in nonphysical arenas such as the activities of our mind, attitudes and emotions, and our approach to realizing goals and ambitions.

Why? Because on the surface, it makes sense. It makes so much sense that we find it difficult to hear performance experts when they challenge what we've been taking for granted for so long. "Stop. Wait. You're going about this the wrong way. You're putting in all this extra effort, but you're not getting extra return from it."

But, as loud as these words might be, they're soon drowned out by a persistent little voice in our head that urges us to grind away, persevere, sacrifice. It stirs us with macho maxims like "no pain, no gain" and "put your nose to the grindstone," reminding us of those legions of motivational johnny-come-latelies who, after climbing a mountain or winning a sporting trophy, have presumed the authority to trot out endless clichés about perseverance and effort.

Yet, while all this is happening, you keep asking yourself why things aren't changing. Why are you working harder but not getting ahead? Why is it that no matter how hard you try to please, you end up pleasing no one, least of all yourself?

So much for the hard way.

Hard questions about "the hard way"

Why is it that the harder you concentrate on your tennis serve or golf swing, the worse it turns out?

Why is it that the harder you try to solve a problem or remember a phone number, the further away from the answer you get?

Why is it that you're working harder and longer, yet you aren't getting further ahead?

If getting your life into balance were just a matter of time and concentration, why can't you do it just by working out a schedule?

After all this hard work and effort, how come you still sit down and ask, "Why am I doing all this? What's it all for?"

Or do it the Calm Way™

Be honest now: Deep down, have you ever had the feeling that there might be a better way to get ahead than just more hard slog?

Think back. Were your instincts telling you that if you just slowed down and relaxed a little, you might achieve a better result?

In so many fields this is now being shown to be true. Certainly the more enlightened sporting coaches have discovered it. Martial artists have always known it. The best therapists instinctively know it, as do musicians and actors. In fact, more and more successful people are now discovering that the best performance comes not from applying more exertion, but less.

Yes, less.

Now that you're thinking about it, you may recall having seen this demonstrated. How often have you seen individuals produce impressive feats or achievements—sporting, artistic, academic, or commercial—without any apparent strain or struggle? How often have you seen great insights and creativity from the young and carefree? How often have you seen the relaxed competitor outperform the tense one? How often have you seen the less-experienced colleague produce more exciting solutions than the hardworking pros?

It happens all the time. More important, it happens far more predictably than you may have suspected.

This is the knowledge that underpins the Calm Way.

If you choose, you can put the hard way behind you forever. You can let go and discover a more easygoing approach to achieving what you want. Discover how to lift your performance as you maintain a state of inner calm. Learn how to bring more balance into your life at the same time as you take it easier.

> The Calm Way: The more relaxed your approach to finding balance, the easier it is to achieve.

You don't need years of training for this. Nor do you need any particular talents or natural abilities. All you need is the Calm Way, a few simple techniques, and the discipline to take this more relaxed approach to life.

So, sit back, kick off your shoes, and see where this takes you. We're on a journey now—a pleasurable one if you wish it to be—during which you will discover how to:

- achieve more in all avenues of life, without investing any more time
- balance your responsibilities between work, home, and the rest of your world
- get more enjoyment from what you do
- find more time for yourself and your relationships.

All this without strain and with minimal effort.

The key to using this book

The fact that you're reading a book called *Perfect Balance* suggests that you believe some degree of change may be needed in your immediate world. Whether you consider this to be a slight modification to what already exists or a total makeover, the principles remain the same.

Change usually takes place in one of four ways: imposed change, physical change, mental change, or behavioral change.

IMPOSED change comes from the outside. You get laid off, get married or divorced, have a heart attack, get taken over by a competitor. In the main, there's not a lot you can do about this change; all you can do is respond. Imposed change is often stressful.

PHYSICAL change appeals to the pragmatic folk because it's demonstrable, achievable, and measurable. Do something! Take action! Pull it in, send them out, lift it up, turn them over—almost anything with an action verb applies. But despite its dynamic appeal, there are great limitations to what physical change can achieve when it comes to life balance. Apart from juggling your diary, rearranging your furniture, or changing the ergonomics of your work environment, there may not be a lot you can do.

MENTAL change can involve shifts of attitude, belief, and/or motivation. While not as measurable as physical change, it is far more effective in the longer term. You can bring this about through conscious effort, as well as by methods that work on the unconscious mind, such as repetition or suggestion.

BEHAVIORAL change usually stems from mental change combined, perhaps, with the development of new skills. Substituting new, more beneficial behaviors is the most powerful way to overcome more limiting ones.

Much of this book focuses on the area where you have a real

power to effect change: the "mental" category. Because for most people, perfect balance is more a state of mind than it is a state of circumstances. You will accomplish most by concentrating on your attitudes, emotions and perspectives, with slightly less emphasis on your behavior and even less on physical change.

Whatever approach you take to making this change, you will find the techniques and strategies in the pages ahead. If you prefer to work through these in a logical, sequential way, you'll find this book is structured accordingly. Alternatively, you may arrive at the same end in a more intuitive way, and find what you're looking for after just a few steps. This sometimes occurs because you already have the solutions you are seeking. You may not be fully conscious of this yet, but much of what you need for perfect balance is well within your mental reach right now.

> The Calm Way: Everything you need for a perfectly balanced life you already have. There's nothing new you need; there's nothing you have to give up. All you have to do is rediscover and refocus the strengths you have now.

The challenges of thinking like a manager

If you work in management or have a managerial role, you may have another challenge to contend with. Often this brings with it a "management style" of thinking—an analytical, methodical, and unemotional way of dealing with information.

Invariably, this is accompanied by an overreliance on the senses—"If I can't see, hear, touch, taste, or smell it, it can't exist"—and facts.

How many times have you said or heard one of your colleagues say, "Just show me the data"?

As useful as this type of thinking may be at an organizational level, it's not much use on a personal level. You are already aware of its limitations. Through your own experience you've discovered that no amount of information or data can make you feel easier about your ever-increasing workload and responsibilities. You've discovered that no amount of discipline or willpower can help you to feel happier, more peaceful, or more content with your life. And that no amount of management skills can bring even the most basic level of balance to your life. Clearly, this is going to take something more.

So, if you feel that you have a "management thinking style," I'd like to ask something of you: For the duration of this book give yourself permission to forget being in charge and allow your instincts to play a role. Give yourself permission to rely more on what you sense and feel than on what you think you know. Give yourself permission to rely more on your intuition than on data. Give yourself permission to forget about the map and to enjoy the journey.

You'll be delighted at how far this will take you.

This book has only one purpose: to help you find perfect balance.

Once you have attained that state, the book's purpose ceases.
It's unlikely you will ever need to retrace your steps.

So keep a pen handy, and use these pages as a record of your journey.
Make notes on them. Underline. Doodle. Write your lists directly onto
the page. Turn this book into a journal.

Then you'll have a permanent reminder of what a good time
you had finding your way here.

What a good idea!

2.

Where did the balance go?

There used to be balance in your life.

You used to rise when you felt like it, eat only what you fancied and tip the rest on the carpet, play with the toys you liked, stare out the window at nothing in particular, nap when you felt like it, bawl when you were bored, and wet your pants whenever the urge took you. Yes, life was balanced then.

It wasn't so many years ago that life seemed more balanced for adults as well. You knew who the good guys were. You knew what was healthy and what was not. You knew your place in the world. You had a clear idea of what was expected of you and what you could expect in return. You knew the difference between work and play, and you had time for both. You even had a fair idea of what lay ahead as you aged and retired in an orderly fashion. And, above all, you knew that the harder you worked, the easier things were going to get.

That was only a few generations back. People felt that life was easier and more balanced then. So why should we feel so different today?

For a start, the overwhelming expectation of that era was that life was going to become easier and more balanced in the future. By contrast, today's expectation is that life is going to be harder and less balanced in the future.

Why the big change?

Some blame it on demographics, a crazy mixture of urban congestion and the changing family unit. Prior to the 1970s the average household included a full-time breadwinner and a full-time homemaker—well-defined roles that provided a degree of certainty and order. Today single-person households are increasingly common, and almost everyone is a breadwinner.

Some say it's because today is an age of extremes, where wild fluctuations in diet, entertainment, behavior, and work practices are so commonplace that we hardly recognize them as extremes anymore.

Some blame it on the intrusiveness of the media. E-mail. Spam. Pornography. Advertising. Reality TV. Cable. Satellite. SMS. Mobile technology.

Some say it's the length of the workday. After a century of steadily decreasing work hours, we've had a rapid upturn in the past two decades. With the possible exception of France, which a decade ago reduced the official workweek, all developed countries have recorded substantial increases in the hours worked each week. On average, full-time employees work at least three hours longer each week today than in the 1980s.

Some say it's role confusion. Are we breadwinners, homemakers, or both? Or neither? Are we employees first, or are we managers, parents, or lovers? Should we seek out new jobs or relationships rather than trying to make existing ones more satisfying?

Some say it's because we're doing too much. Too much work.

Too much study. Too much ambition. Too much structure in our recreation activities. Too many skills and qualifications. Too much focus on growth. Too much complexity in relationships. Too much consumption. Too much, too much.

Some say it's because we're not doing enough! Not paying enough attention to our health and relationships because we're working too hard. Not focusing enough on our work because there are too many distractions in our personal life. Not earning enough. Not loving enough. Not getting enough sex. Not getting enough sleep. Not enough, not enough.

My opinion is it's probably a combination of all of the above.

But whatever the reasons for feeling your life is out of balance, you can take comfort in the fact that you're not alone. It's a sentiment that underpins most of the restlessness and dissatisfaction in the developed world.

Balance overcomes restlessness

One of the most rewarding discoveries that awaits you in this book is that having a sense of balance in life removes much, if not most, of the restlessness. But, at this very moment, balance may seem to you like a hazy, unattainable state. We notice this a lot at our public programs when we ask, "What does it mean to have a well-balanced life?"

On the surface, a simple-enough question. But, strangely, one that very few people can answer with any degree of insight. Overwhelmingly, they will relate it to how much work they're doing or how much pressure they're under. But there's a lot more to balance than this.

To add to the confusion, "life balance" is frequently one of those fuzzy promises made by promoters as an inevitable extension of their particular product or belief. You may have encountered examples such as the following:

- Many corporate training companies cobble together little programs designed to fulfill some ideal known as work–life balance.
- The stress-management industry claims that by overcoming stress you'll get your life into balance.
- Labor representatives say balance will happen when employers reduce their demands on, and provide more benefits for, their employees.
- Personal trainers promise that once you get your waistline and pectorals in shape you'll discover real balance.
- Most religions claim that when you get your spiritual life in order your life will have balance.
- Romance magazines say it will happen when you find your true soulmate. Pornographers promise a variation on this.

For an issue that's so frequently spoken about, "life balance" is a difficult concept to define in a positive context. It's much easier to explain and understand it in the negative—when life gets out of balance. Later you'll read about some of the people we spoke to while researching this book. They'll tell you about the lack of balance in their lives. Some of their stories will seem familiar.

There's balance in your life when . . .	There's imbalance in your life when . . .
Work, home, friends, and other interests all seem to dovetail seamlessly.	Your habits and behaviors limit your satisfaction from the other parts of your life.
Your personal priorities are in harmony with your work priorities.	Your personal priorities conflict with your work priorities.
The moment you arrive home, you're in a "home frame of mind."	You see home as a place to recharge before work the next day.
Your personal life complements your work life, and vice versa.	You depend on one part of your life to compensate for the shortcomings in another.
You relax and enjoy work, home, and the company of others.	You bring home your work tension or concerns at the end of each day.
You quickly recover from setbacks.	With every setback, your life seems less in control.
You're enjoying yourself in what you do, and you feel useful.	You go through the motions and don't get any fun out of it anymore.
You feel content, unhurried, and not overly worried by events.	There are so many things on your plate you don't know where to turn.
You perform your duties smoothly and effortlessly, and enjoy every moment of them.	You think there simply aren't enough hours in the day to accomplish what you want in life.
All aspects of your life seem in place, and everything makes sense.	You have it all, but you still don't feel satisfied.

The balance you crave

If you're going to bring more balance to your life, it will help to look more closely at what this state is meant to be. The traditional way of looking at balance is sometimes called the "Either-Or" perspective.

In this sense, balance is a state in which two opposing elements or forces, of equal weight or importance, effectively cancel each other out and become stable. Or, it's where one element is rearranged to offset or counter the influence of another.

When you apply the Either-Or perspective to your life, it's always colored by the issues of the day. The opposing forces will be the immediate conflict areas of your life.

- If you believe you're working too hard, the opposing forces will probably be work and rest. Or hard work and fun.
- If you're feeling guilty about not spending enough time with your family, the opposing forces may be career and home.
- If you're spending too many nights in clubs and are at risk of losing your job, the opposing forces may be professional life and private life.

• If you've just caught sight of your "love handles" in the changing room mirror, the opposing forces may be calorie intake and exercise.

Following the Either-Or perspective to its logical conclusion, you would assume that once you got those two opposing forces in balance, your life would be in balance.

Unfortunately, life is never that simple—because there are always more than two opposing forces.

A balanced whole

The ideal state of life balance—*perfect* balance, if you like—occurs when all the different forces and influences in your life are contained within a satisfying and harmonious whole. Nothing is out of proportion and no one element is emphasized at the expense of the others.

Not only does this take into account the immediate conflict areas of your life (work and home, for example), it accommodates the rest of "you"—your work and your play, your needs and your responsibilities, your hopes and ambitions, your spiritual needs, your mental health and physical health.

When you reach this state, your life suddenly seems as if it has shape and direction. You get more satisfaction from what you do. You have more energy. You're more capable of making sound decisions. You feel you have more time at your disposal. You feel centered and content. You feel whole. And, best of all, you find you have a healthy new perspective on the pressures and responsibilities in your life.

> The Calm Way: Perfect balance is not achieved by abandoning certain
> areas of your life, but by integrating them so all your interests, needs,
> and responsibilities merge into one harmonious whole.

Clearly, to achieve such a life-changing result is going to take more than simply offsetting one pressure against another. And it takes more than rearranging or redistributing two pressures—say, work and home. If you want to feel like a complete, perfectly balanced individual, you need to approach it holistically.

In science, the holistic view sees the world or universe as an undivided whole, where all parts are interconnected and relevant. In relation to you, a holistic view sees you as an undivided whole—body, mind, and spirit—where each is interconnected, vital, and relevant. This view is essential to achieving perfect balance. It takes into account *all* the forces and influences in your life: your work and play, your career and family, your physical and spiritual health, your needs and responsibilities, your dreams and aspirations, and the contributions you make to the world around you.

The many forces in your life

If your life consisted of only one set of interests and responsibilities—say, work and career—you'd find it relatively easy to maintain a sense of order and perspective.

But you have many sets of interests and responsibilities. Sometimes they pull in opposing directions. At any given time, as well as having to satisfy your own needs, you also have to deal with the needs and expectations of others—your family, your employer, your friends, your neighbors and social groups, not to mention your community and the government.

Perfect balance occurs when all these interests, needs, and responsibilities coexist comfortably and harmoniously:

- personal needs and ambitions
- family responsibilities and duties
- work responsibilities
- professional obligations
- social obligations
- community responsibilities
- moral or spiritual obligations
- imaginary obligations.

These tend to fall into one of four motivating categories that are generally seen as two sets of opposing forces: Physical opposing Spiritual, and Work opposing Social. (There are dozens of subcategories that could also be considered, but, in the main, most of your life's influences and activities will be covered by these four.) When one side competes against the other, you have tension, and this contributes to what you sense as an imbalance in your life.

PHYSICAL relates to all your worldly needs and comforts—health, food, security, recreation, sleep, sex.

Physical contrasts with . . .

SPIRITUAL is not just God-related stuff, but also life values, the search for meaning, the need to make a difference, and the need to help others or even the planet.

WORK is mostly your occupation, but it also involves a range of mental needs, such as the desire to achieve and produce, and the desire for personal growth, recognition, respect, and self-esteem.

Work contrasts with . . .

SOCIAL encompasses all of your human interactions—family, home, friends, and community involvements.

If you focus too much on any one category, you will find that its opposing category is neglected to some degree. Too much focus on your work will usually mean some sort of compromise in the "social" part of your life—your relationships and home life. Too much focus on the physical side of your world will usually mean the spiritual side—such as the search for meaning or the need to make a difference—has been downplayed.

The ideal is a balanced, harmonious whole, where all parts are interconnected and relevant, and no parts compete with one another. Naturally, we must take a few steps before we reach that stage.

The first is to determine what your life looks like now.

Theoretically, when your life is perfectly balanced, you will pay equal attention to your Physical, Social, Spiritual, and Work needs and responsibilities. So if you were to graph the emphasis of your life, you'd favor no one category over another, and you would mark a circle in the middle of each line. It would look more or less like (a) below.

Of course, this doesn't take into account that each of us is an individual, with personal tastes, drives, and motivations. So the graph of your ideal could look different from this. For example, your Work-Social emphasis might be centrally placed between these coordinates, but your Physical-Spiritual emphasis might skew more toward Spiritual, as shown in (b) below.

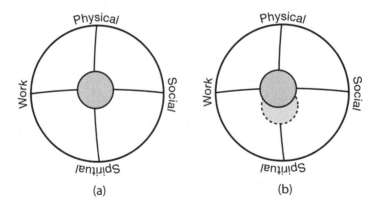

(a) (b)

Even though you might pursue a harmonious, holistic spread between each of the categories, in everyday life this ideal is seldom achieved—as you'll see from the stories of the people we interviewed while researching this book.

A study in imbalance

(Note: In each of the following case studies, it is the interviewee—not me—who believes their life needs more balance.)

When people think or speak of things being out of balance, they're not usually referring to a *slight* imbalance between areas, but massive tilts in one direction or another—in other words, extremes of the Either-Or perspective described earlier.

Extremes of any kind produce undesirable results. All protein and no carbohydrates leads to ill health. All television and no exercise leads to an expanding waistline. All sex and no love leads to frustration and emptiness. All talking and no listening leads to ignorance. All work and no play makes Jack a dull boy.

It is this last area—all work and no play—that probably interests most readers of this book. This is the classic tension area between the Work and Social areas of your life. Often this takes place without your ever noticing it.

Such was the case with Ms. A.

 **Ms. A is the divisional director of a financial services institution.** With a demanding role in a stressful industry, Ms. A is in a similar position to most of today's senior executives: outstanding at work, less than successful at home.

As much as she tries not to, she invariably brings home the stress of her "normal" workday. She just can't turn off when she leaves the office, and she has learned to live with work pressure twenty-four hours a day. There's a name for this. At the Calm Centre, we call it embedded tension: accumulated stress, tension, fear, and doubt from one part of your life being carried into other unrelated parts.

There are two by-products of embedded tension. First, it makes it next to impossible for you to relax and enjoy the nonwork aspects of life. Second, it desensitizes you to the impact your stress has on others.

Ms. A grudgingly admits to the former. It is difficult for her to relax and enjoy the little things that used to mean so much to her. But she takes exception to the "desensitizing" part.

"They know I have a demanding job," she argues. "But they also know I can't wait to come home to them in the evening. It's the one thing I look forward to."

Even her youngest child suspects that what Ms. A loves to come home to is not so much them, as any place that's not work. A place where she can turn off and recharge her batteries before heading back to the fray the next day.

It's easy to see that Ms. A's work has taken over her life. So much so that she sometimes sees her extra-curricular roles, such as being a mother, as another duty to fulfill rather than an activity to enjoy.

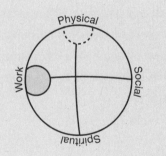

This graph shows the present emphasis of Ms. A's life "balance." If you compare it to the ideal on page 29, you'll see how her concentration on Work is achieved at the expense of her relationships (Social), her more spiritually oriented needs, and, to a lesser extent, her day-to-day Physical needs.

Although Ms. A may never have consciously made the decision to let work take over her life this way, her ambition has allowed it to continue.

Ambition is fairly easy to understand, and it can be moderated. But what happens when work issues dominate your life and there is little ambition involved?

Mr. B is a senior lecturer at a major university. Mr. B's career has taken a turn for the worse. He believes it is the result of his age, since the plum positions seem to be offered to colleagues much younger and less experienced than himself.

He is struggling to overcome his latest setback: not only was he passed over for a position he applied for, but he was moved to a smaller office on a less-convenient campus.

"It's insulting," he explains. "It's as if all my experience counts for nothing."

Mr. B has discovered that at a stage of life when things are supposed to be getting easier, the pressure is actually increasing. More and more he is taking home his work tensions and concerns. He's made a conscious effort to avoid this, but with little success. Increasingly, he feels guilty about a predicament that is not of his making.

Driven by a mix of righteousness and insecurity, Mr. B doubles his work efforts in an endeavor to prove his worth. Now he is working harder than ever before.

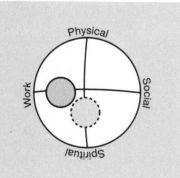

Moreover, he is doing this at the expense of his home life, his relationship with his partner, Debbie, as well as his golf, which used to give him pleasure just a few months ago.

Compare the emphasis on Mr. B's balance graph with the ideal on page 29.

The Calm Way: There's not a single additional thing
you have to do to find perfect balance.
In fact, you may choose to do even less.

Productivity

If we're talking about work-life imbalance—as opposed to a broader
life imbalance—one of the greatest contributors is the quest for
improved productivity.

To appreciate how this has got out of hand, you need only examine the change in approach of big organizations over the past few
decades.

The dynamics of any externally focused organization is simple:
one arm brings the money in, and the other arm shuffles it around.
(Even if it is a government department, a church, or a charity, money
is usually the central part of the equation.) Or, to put it another way:
one arm provides the service, while the second arm supports or manages the first.

It wasn't very long ago—certainly in my working lifetime—that
the most influential arm of an enterprise was the former, the one that
brought the money in. Then, in the 1980s, the second arm started
to flex its muscles. Instead of focusing on what was coming in, the
organization started to focus on how it could maximize this income.
The call was for improved productivity. The rationale was that by
improving productivity you directly influence the bottom line.

From a human perspective, improving productivity means you
have to do one of two things:
- produce more at the same cost
- produce the same at reduced cost.

Either way, the result is the same: added pressure for the person who's meant to be producing. The worker. The team. The department. Because whenever you seek to increase output or reduce cost without changing employee levels or introducing new technology, you create pressure. This pressure, if not properly addressed, flows over to other aspects of life.

 **Ms. C is human resources manager of a legal firm. Last night she counted 163 tasks that she had to complete by the end of the week. Ms. C's employers** consider her one of their best. She does her job superbly, never complains, and is continually seeking ways to advance herself.

Recently, the nature of her work began to change. Her firm merged with a similar-sized competitor. The purpose? Economies of scale and reduction in overheads. With the flourish of a pen, the number of people for whom she was responsible almost doubled. Yet her team levels remained the same. (The HR executives of the other firm were made redundant.) Her responsibilities increased in other ways. Mergers mean duplicated positions, which mean layoffs and outplacement tasks, all of which contributed to Ms. C's workload. She made a case for additional resources, but it was pointed out that hiring new staff was counter to the objective of reducing overheads, which was after all the purpose of the merger. For the first time in her working life, Ms. C feels that she is losing control.

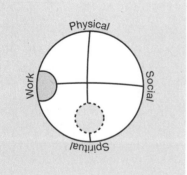

Ms. C is concerned about the stress she is working under and the fact that her world is dominated by her work. In an effort to broaden her interests and add more balance to her life, she is undertaking a variety of different professional courses. As well, she has joined two industry bodies and committees and is standing for election to a third.

As you can see from the graph, adding these new interests to her life has not produced the balance she desires.

 **Mr. C, husband of Ms. C, is an executive in a group that manages large shopping centers.** While Mr. C does not feel quite as overwhelmed by his occupation as his wife does by hers, his life is similar. It is dominated by work. His work, her work, and things that they are working toward.

"We're always saying we have to get off this treadmill," he confesses, "but we can't afford it right now."

The Cs do not plan to have children, and both believe they must put in the effort they do if they are to be comfortable later in life. They've expressed the desire to retire "early" and then take life easier. In line with this, they seem unusually preoccupied with the high cost of retirement and of life expectancies—issues that people their age will not encounter for decades to come.

The imbalance in Mr. C's life is not unlike that of his wife. The major difference is that, where she "copes" with work pressure by taking on additional studies and industry roles, he relies on alcohol in an attempt to deal with the stresses. As a result, the graph of his life imbalance skews more to the physical.

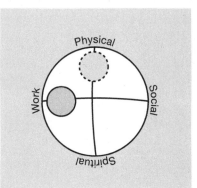

The Calm Way: The safest way to get off the treadmill is to slow it down.
Slow down.

So little time, so much to do

Ask anyone in the workplace what the main cause of imbalance is in their life, and nine times out of ten they'll come up with the same answer: time.

As the world gets busier, productivity expectations grow, workplace and lifestyle demands increase, and the needs of your friends and family become more insistent; there's no escaping the fact that the one thing you need more of is time.

More time to do what you have to do. Or fewer things to do in the time you have available. Which brings us to the second-most complained-about topic in today's workplace: workload. Or, as it is more often described: overwork. Both are related to time.

Ironically, overwork doesn't stem from having to do too much work. It stems from trying to squeeze too many things into a specific period of time. If you had an extra twelve working hours and the same amount of work to do, chances are you wouldn't consider yourself overworked. Once you've narrowed the problem down to too many demands being made on your available time, it becomes an easier matter to solve. But sometimes it is solved at a price.

Mr. D owns and runs an accountancy practice of nine employees. Mr. D's life is his business. His first thoughts each day are usually to do with work—the invoices he has to revise during the day, the junior he has to lay off, the coffee machine he has to replace, the . . . "Oh, you mean it's Saturday?"

When he comes home in the evening, he tries not to think of work—the client he seems to be losing or the refinancing proposal he has to read before morning—as he tries to be an interesting dinner companion for his wife.

He also desperately wants to be an attentive father. On Saturday mornings he takes the kids to soccer, then the rest of the day is spent going over the accounts and preparing for Monday morning's meetings.

"There may be financial compensations in having your own business, but you pay a price for them. The price of failure is not just lost income; it could be losing all the family assets. What would my family do then? Sometimes I ask myself why I bother. Then a bill comes in for the school fees, or my wife's car needs to be repaired, or the swimming pool needs resurfacing—and I realize I don't have any choice."

Mr. D genuinely wants to devote more time to his family, and he feels guilty about not being able to do so. But fear prevents him from making the decisions that would allow this. His combination of guilt and fear is a toxic mix, which, left unaddressed, will further upset the balance in his life.

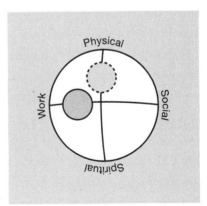

A matter of choice

We like to believe that the pressure in our life is created by others—our employer, partner, children, client, coach, coworkers, the taxman, or government. In reality, however, it is usually self-imposed, the result of our own drives, beliefs, ambitions, or work practices.

The more pressure you're under, the harder this will be to see. You may genuinely believe that your "sacrifices" are essential for the well-being of your family, business, colleagues, or community. You may believe you have no control over these matters and that you are obliged to do what you do. Dr. E sincerely believed this was the admission price for being in her profession.

 **Dr. E is a fashionable obstetrician, delivering 250+ babies each year.** Dr. E delivers more celebrities' babies than any other obstetrician around. In the early years, she relished this success. Now she believes she is the victim of it. It follows her everywhere and is especially intrusive in her home life. She acknowledges this is unfair to her husband and teenage children, but she cannot see a way out.

"It really does wear me down," she sighs. "I'm on call twenty-four hours a day. Weekends, dinner parties, funerals . . . it doesn't matter, they'll track me down. My patients *expect* me to be accessible at all times. They need me."

Dr. E takes comfort in the fact that it is the nature of obstetrics to be at the mercy of mothers-to-be. There are, however, clear professional choices she can make that could reduce this pressure. Foremost among these is the number of patients she accepts; simply by reducing this to the 150–200 deliveries some of her colleagues accept as a limit, she would automatically restore some balance.

The fact that she agrees to such a punishing number of deliveries is unlikely to be either profession- or lifestyle-related. It is more to do with self-image—or pride, if you like. Like so many other successful people, Dr. E is attached to her accomplishments.

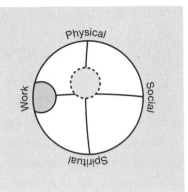

Feeling in control

The less control you feel you exert over your immediate world, the more likely you are to suffer some degree of stress, fear, anxiety, or anger in relation to it.

The Calm Way: You master the events that affect your life not by trying to control or change the events but by changing the way you respond to them.

Any number of workplace situations can produce this feeling—having to perform monotonous and repetitive tasks, lack of communication, inadequate job descriptions, dictatorial supervisors, an overwhelming workload—yet it relates to more areas than just work. Ill health can produce the same feeling. So can physical conditions such as obesity. And undesirable habits. And financial problems. And relationship issues. But most complex of all is when a number of these factors occur at the same time.

Ms. F is the fifty-two-year-old caregiver to her invalid husband and personal assistant to the CEO of a transport company. For almost fifteen years, Ms. F has been personal assistant to the CEO. It is a powerful position, one that allows a strong sense of autonomy and control in her job.

But still she feels that she has little control over her life.

Above all, Ms. F's work is a refuge, an escape from the relentless demands of an ailing husband who suffers from early-onset Alzheimer's disease. Caring for him is more than a difficult job; it's a thankless one as well. Not only does Ms. F's husband fail to recognize what she does for him, he frequently fails to even recognize her.

"There are so many times I just want to stay in bed all day—because the moment he lays eyes on me, I'll be in for the same thing over and over again. The same questions. The same puppy-dog stalking. And what's

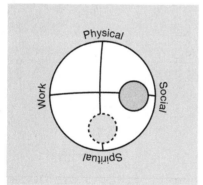

hardest of all to take is seeing my bright, full-of-life husband slowly losing his mind."

Despite the sense of autonomy she enjoys in her job, Ms. F cannot escape the lack of control she feels in her personal life. Even more frustrating, no amount of effort or planning seems to influence this.

Competing priorities and responsibilities

How's this for an ideal world. . . .

You have only one priority in your life to focus on. Just one. So while everyone else is running around concentrating on their work, their children, their waistline, their qualifications, their tennis serve, and their father's illness, you just have to concentrate on one. Whatever that might be.

Wouldn't that be a luxury?

But, reality being what it is, there are probably more priorities in your life than one. More than you'd ever thought of or asked for.

When these priorities compete for your attention, you have a classic imbalance situation. Because, while focusing your attention on only one thing may be calming and fulfilling, dividing your attention creates tension and unease.

One of the most common examples of competing priorities relates to working parents, especially solo parents, or when one parent carries most of the child-raising responsibilities. Such roles entail a myriad of time and economic and emotional burdens—often with no simple answers to managing them.

Traditionally, women have been more affected by this in the workplace. Not just because there are more women who carry dual-role responsibilities, but because there can be not-so-subtle expectations that they will do it naturally and easily. However, as you'll see with Mr. G, it can also apply to men.

Mr. G is a father of two, caregiver to three, and a member of a software design team. Mr. G thought he had it all: an interesting job in an Internet company, a loving partner and son, and then a new baby.

But things changed. Following the birth of their second child, his partner entered into a long period of depression and became unable to care for herself or the children. As a result, Mr. G had to care for her and the children, as well as fulfilling his responsibilities at work.

His supervisor was more than accommodating. Having experienced such pressures herself at one time, she suggested a more flexible work program, urging Mr. G to use a laptop and do more work from home.

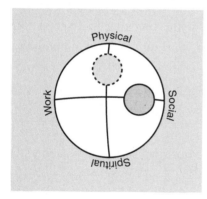

"I can't understand the reaction of my teammates. A man going home early to look after his kids . . . I think they think I'm using this as an excuse for not pulling my weight."

So he overcompensates. He volunteers for tasks that would normally have been shared among the team. He returns to the office most evenings after the children have gone to bed. He works alternate weekends. In total, Mr. G is now working longer hours, and taking on more responsibilities, than he did when he was in the office full-time.

Divided responsibilities can lead to feeling frustrated and pressured. In Mr. G's case, this was compounded by a sense of responsibility he felt toward the team of which he was a member. This was every bit as pressing as the responsibility he felt toward his employer and family.

Blurred boundaries

Another contributor to Mr. G's unease is the constant overlapping of work and private roles.

For most of us, there are fairly well-defined boundaries between work and the rest of our life. But, more and more, these boundaries are being blurred. With extended work hours, e-mail, mobile phones, laptop computers, not to mention the proliferation of relationships that begin in the workplace, the overlap of work and private life is ever-increasing.

Having unambiguous boundaries, where it's clear how your different life roles relate to one another, is a major step toward feeling balanced and productive in the life you lead. As you read this book, you will discover how these boundaries fall into place as your life becomes more balanced.

What drives you?

Motivation is the "Why?" in life. When you decide there is something you must achieve, motivation provides the energy for you to achieve it. It's what encourages you to go the extra distance, to overcome adversity, to succeed.

You also need motivation to establish balance in your life.

There's no shortage of motivation in the workplace; almost all successful people have it, as do all people who are striving to be successful. But frequently the motivation you have at work stays there when you go home at night. After a stressful day, it's all you can manage just to fire up the microwave and turn on the television. Where is your energy and motivation now?

Worse, if that lack of energy and motivation begins to spread, and you end up taking it back into the workplace the following day, it could be an indication of burnout, a psychological and often physical condition that stems from extended periods of stress.

From an employer's perspective, burnout is doubly harmful because it tends to strike the most valuable employees of an organization—those who will go "above and beyond," working longer and harder without hesitation or complaint.

There is a range of manifestations of this condition, but you'll recognize it by the evaporation of drive and motivation. When burnout occurs, you find yourself going through the motions at work, without deriving any of the stimulation or satisfaction. Some people find it difficult even to go through the motions.

Mr. H is a prime example of this.

Mr. H is a tired newspaper columnist. When he looks back over his career, all Mr. H sees is an unbroken line of deadlines. For two decades: every lead followed, every deadline met, every editorial expectation satisfied.

He was a driven reporter. His obsession with fairness, truth, and making a difference flourished throughout his thirties. It peaked in his early forties—then his life began to change.

He was too busy to notice. Too busy to see how the ongoing nature of his work denied him a sense of accomplishment. All he noticed was that no sooner had one corruption been exposed, no sooner had today's issue gone to press, than the next one was due. The next one was always due. There were no spaces in his life. But, yes, there were many cigarettes, double espressos, and glasses of red wine to help keep the pressures at bay.

Mr. H resolved to slow down after his bypass surgery. But it's not easy to walk away from the drives and habits of half a lifetime. Instead of slowing down, things seemed to speed up. Everywhere he turned, every time the phone rang, he watched television or met a stranger at the train station—a potential story. There was no letup. His whole life was a potential story. He couldn't escape it.

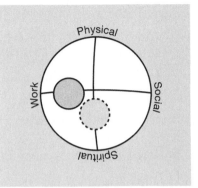

Then, out of the blue, everything changed. It wasn't so much a conscious effort to slow down as a realization after the event. He found it harder and harder to get started each day. Soon he was making excuses, cutting corners, falling back on old story angles he'd used decades ago.

"Can't seem to get into it anymore. To be honest, it's bloody boring. Nothing new. I've done it all before. I know what people are going to say before they say it; I feel I could write the story without doing a single interview. Maybe it's this cold getting me down. [Mr. H has been sniffling throughout the interview.] Can't seem to shake it."

It's not difficult to see the imbalance in Mr. H's life. Of more immediate concern is that he's suffering from burnout, brought about by years of unrelenting hard work and commitment, combined with a lack of attention to his own well-being.

Goals and ambitions

Some years ago I was involved in music production. One of my employees—a guitarist—was one of the most unflappable people I'd ever worked with. No work situation ever fazed him. If a session ran into problems, or a backing player failed to turn up, or he got caught in the traffic on the way to the studio, he wouldn't miss a beat.

I was intrigued by how he could remain so centered while there was so much pressure all around him. I suspect it was a matter of ambition. He was determined to be known as the best in his field, and he pursued this goal to the exclusion of almost everything else—patiently, singlemindedly, and without strain. If anything went wrong or activities didn't go according to plan, his goal was always there in front of him keeping him on course. This is what gave his life purpose and led him to believe his life was well balanced.

> The Calm Way: It's impossible to impose order on the physical world. It's much easier to attain an orderly frame of mind, which is much more powerful and sustainable in the long run.

Knowing exactly what your goals and priorities are makes it easier for you to find balance. But if you're hazy about these or try to focus on several areas at once, you'll find it difficult to keep them all in perspective.

Ms. I is a full-time homemaker and mother to a six-year-old and a toddler. Some consider it the height of luxury to be able to stay home and look after your children full-time. Ms. I regularly reminds herself of this fact.

Her friends in the workforce envy the life she leads. In turn, Ms. I envies theirs. She envies their stimulating environment, their adult company, and their freedom. She envies the fact that they're capitalizing on their education and experience to build meaningful careers for themselves. She can't stop thinking about how all-consuming her homemaker role has become and about the career she used to have.

As Ms. I's envy turns to dissatisfaction, she overeats. And puts on weight. And allows her discontent to affect her family.

"Did you know I was one of the top stage managers in the country?

Whenever a major show would come to town, I'd be the first person they'd try to get on their crew. It took so much to get my career to that stage, it's almost criminal not to take advantage of it."

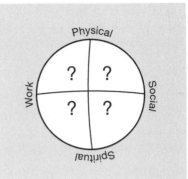

The imbalance and discontent in Ms. I's life is driven by her conflict of ambitions: on the one hand she wants to spend time with her children, and on the other she wants to nurture the career she's invested so many years in. A balanced approach may be to have them both—in more or less equal proportions.

Having clear goals provides more than direction. It gives you a sense of autonomy and being in control of your life. It's not everything, of course; Ms. J is an example of how you can feel in control of your world yet still feel like there's something missing.

Ms. J is a mother of three children and a successful market research executive. To an outsider, Ms. J has the best of all worlds: excellent health, three bright children, a loving husband, a housekeeper and nanny, a successful career, and all the trappings of affluence.

All the parts of her world are seemingly in order. She's achieved all she ever hoped for, and more. Yet in spite of all this, she is dissatisfied. She feels something is not right. Something is missing. And, worse, this restlessness is beginning to affect those around her.

"A lot of the time I feel really miserable, and there's no good reason for it. My sister said it might be depression. I don't think so. I think it's just that my life is so extraordinarily shallow."

The longer the interview goes on, the more distaste Ms. J reveals for

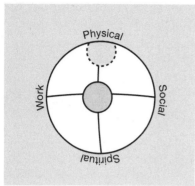

the values of her immediate world. She lists many things she despairs of: the decline in community standards, the growing competitiveness in life, the materialistic pressures that influence her family. But, in every instance, she brings the conversation back to herself.

"You must think I'm dreadfully self-absorbed talking this way. Especially when there are so many more important things we should be worrying about."

The more Ms. J and her family achieve and accomplish, the more she feels her life is imbalanced. The gap between her Physical and Spiritual needs grows wider. She is neglecting the part of her makeup that relates to values, meaning, and making a difference.

An overdose of spirit

You will have seen many examples of the imbalance such as that experienced by Ms. J. But what about the opposite? Can you imagine how, in this nonstop world, someone's life imbalance could be skewed toward "too much Spiritual, not enough Physical"? I must confess that when I began researching this book I thought such people would be difficult to find. Yet at least one of the people we interviewed turned out to be in this category.

Mr. K is a man of many causes. Mr. K works as an auditor in a local government department involved with soil and water conservation. That's his day job. However, his interest is not his job, it's . . . well, it's many things.

He's a paid member of the Democratic Party. He's worked for Amnesty International, collected for Greenpeace, and has marched for animal rights, for refugee rights, against globalization, against the building of high-rise apartments, and against the clearing of old-growth forests.

On paper, Mr. K is passionate about a multitude of causes that relate to the betterment of humankind. There are so many areas where a man like him could make a difference. But instead of being uplifted by feelings of compassion and altruism, he is depressed by what he sees as the ills of the modern world.

"I'm sickened by what we're doing to our planet. Not just big things like the ozone layer, but smaller things like plastic bags. Just a few minutes of use, and they can take up to a thousand years to break down. You know how many birds, whales, seals, and dolphins these kill each year?"

Mr. K is so consumed by his environmental causes that he neglects other aspects of his life. His diet is ill-considered. His work is perfunctory. The only exercise he takes is a short walk to the bus stop each day. And he is so disillusioned by the apathy of workmates and acquaintances that he limits all social contact to environmental campaigners like himself. In short, he is in a rut.

Even though Mr. K pursues his interests with passion and vigor, he gets little enjoyment from them. He sees most of it as work "that has to be done." Compounding this, many of his activities are protest-oriented, negative in nature, and denying any sense of conclusion or fulfillment.

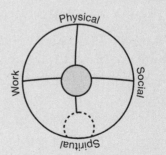

Trapped in the material world

In today's health-conscious, body-conscious, diet-conscious, beauty-conscious world, it's easy to lose sight of the fact that there might be more to being a happy, whole person than just flesh.

True, the physical side of life is important. There are great emotional and physical benefits to be gained from a healthy lifestyle—good diet and regular exercise contribute more to the way you feel than most other activities. But when your focus on diet and exercise becomes obsessive, problems emerge.

Imbalance exists when bookshelves bulge with diet books, when there are more conversations about carbs than foodstuffs, when gyms are more popular than outdoor recreation, when supermarket label-reading takes more time than cooking fresh produce, and when grimacing joggers and power-walkers watch their watches rather than the scenery.

Imbalance also exists when adolescents strive to achieve a certain physical ideal, when adults are disheartened about not having achieved it, and when middle-aged people refuse to accept what nature asserts.

All too often today, the notion of being "healthy" is confused with appearance and physical endurance or performance. Compare that with other perspectives of being healthy, where it's defined as a peaceful, contented state! It may be a coincidence, but as society focuses more and more on body shape, mental health is deteriorating. According to World Health Organization statistics, mental health problems already account for five of the ten major causes of disability in the world. And this proportion is growing.

 **Ms. L is in her early fifties and has been worrying about her physical appearance for as long as she can remember.** Ms. L manages a large reception center, where she is required to dress formally most evenings. She's happy with this because she looks great in an evening dress. Many people comment that she has the looks of a forty-year-old.

These looks come at a price. She has been on one diet or another for over twenty-five years. She runs or power walks at least once a day, goes to the gym five days a week, and hasn't knowingly touched a carbohydrate since she read that they contributed to weight gain. Not that carbohydrates would make that much difference with her, because she's been fighting bulimia since adolescence.

Since her husband left, she's spent a small fortune on plastic-surgery "interventions." Her relationships have consisted of a couple of encounters with gym members. Her only women friends are those she runs or goes to the gym with; she has never seen them outside a training environment. Apart from the times she is training, Ms. L is a lonely and unsatisfied woman.

Ms. L is trapped in her physical world. She exercises out of habit and compulsion rather than enjoyment. Although training and her fitness help her to feel good in a physical sense, the rest of her life is unsatisfying and one-dimensional. But what can she do? Give up the one thing that makes her feel good?

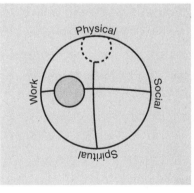

The stress of incompetence

Most of the imbalance stories we covered while preparing this book related to "having to" devote too much time to work at the expense of play or family. But there were some fascinating exceptions. Mr. M's story, for example, related not so much to work levels as competency levels.

 **Mr. M is a well-known executive in the music industry.** As manager and spokesman for a famous rock band, Mr. M got a taste of the limelight at an early age. While this earned him something of a reputation in the music industry, it did nothing to develop his managerial skills.

This became evident not long after he won a prized job as A&R (Artists and Repertoires) manager for a large record company. Within months of signing a string of unsuccessful acts, he knew his days in this talent-developing role were numbered.

"I love the social part of it—the dinners, the parties, the functions. But the moment someone mentions work, I get depressed. It might not look like I've got a lot to do, but it's incredibly stressful. My partner says I should move on. Would you want to give up a job like this?"

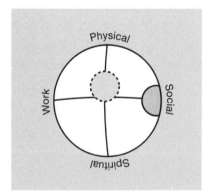

Lack of competence is not often recognized as a major cause of stress in executive ranks. But as Mr. M's story illustrates, lacking the ability to do your job efficiently means you're continually under pressure—a feeling that's difficult to escape at the end of the day.

Imbalance in a nutshell

These stories reveal how life imbalance can be brought about by factors that are not always obvious. Seldom is it the result of external pressure. Often it's the result of choice. Even more often it's the result of psychology or long-held attitudes. But, in every case, the person was most conscious of their life balance when it was no longer there.

This should not be surprising. If your diet consists solely of hamburgers, your dietary imbalance is obvious. If you work eighteen hours a day, your work–life imbalance is obvious. Where it becomes less visible is when you consider it in the broader context of your whole life. Now it becomes a generalized, unsettled feeling. Now it may be the result of not so much what you're doing as what you're *thinking* of doing.

For example, a lot of the imbalance in your life stems from a conflict between the things you want to do and the things you believe you have to do, or what you believe others want you to do.

Imbalance is a feeling or behavior that stems from conflicts between:

- things you *want* to do

- things you *have* to do

- things you *should* do

- things *others* want you to do.

When we were conducting interviews for this book, a sentiment we heard over and over was "I'm doing it for them."

"I work these hours because I'm trying to make a better life for my children."

"If I don't do it, no one else will."

"My team [or patients, students, or clients] depends on me."

"I'd love to play, but my family needs me at home."

"My job responsibilities don't allow it."

"My boss wouldn't tolerate me taking time off."

"Why can't they see that I'm doing it for them?"

Often, when you go to the root of each of these obligations, you find the pressure is self-imposed.

More than any other factor, it is your choices that dictate how well balanced your life is. If you can acknowledge this and accept that the pressure you feel is the result of the choices you make rather than the demands that somebody else makes, you begin to take control. And you're well on the way to perfect balance.

> The Calm Way: You feel more in control when you believe you have choices. It may take a little creativity to see them, but choices exist in every situation.

The conflicts of modern life

Did you ever dream adult life would turn out like this? So many different pressures competing and pulling in different directions at the same time.

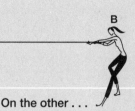

On the one hand . . .	On the other . . .
You're forced to work harder and longer in the quest for productivity.	Your efficiency levels drop because you're working too hard.
Your work demands more and more of your concentration and effort.	Your relationships demand more and more nourishment.
You feel guilty if you don't work as many hours as your colleagues.	You feel guilty for the hours you spend working rather than being with your family and friends.
You have to apply much more effort to get ahead.	You're going nowhere because you neglect your personal development.
You have to work harder so you can afford more leisure and recreation.	Because you work so hard, you have no energy left over to enjoy it.
You squeeze more into your workday so you'll have more time for your family.	You're no fun to be around because you bring home so much stress and frustration.
You need to be mentally and physically fit to be able to accommodate work demands.	Because of work demands, you don't have the time or energy to work on your fitness.
You work harder and longer so that one day you'll have more time for all the creative or spiritual pursuits you've been thinking about.	Because you've worked so hard getting to where you can afford what you want, you have no energy or imagination left to enjoy it.

3.

The big picture

Before you take another step . . .

Here's an important little exercise you can do in your spare time—during breakfast, on the way to work, watching television tonight, or while you're soaking in the tub.

On the surface, this may not seem like it has a lot to do with balance. But it does. And if you do it faithfully, its importance will emerge over the next few days or weeks.

Go out now and get yourself a small note-book, one you can carry around with you wherever you go.

Now, without making too big a deal out of this, make a list of all the good things in your life and all the things you believe are important. Note the virtues and values you believe in.

Finally, record all recreations or fun activities that give you pleasure.

Make this an ongoing exercise while you read this book. Do it at the same time as you put other techniques and methods into practice. The important thing is that you start, and that you start now.

Even if you haven't got the notebook yet, write down ten good things about your life, two human values you admire most, and two recreational activities you love.

How does your life look today?

Do you have a clear picture of the overall shape of your life balance? Most people don't. Yet having such a view is a prerequisite to being able to get to where you want to be.

This chapter is about determining the state of your life balance at this moment, then determining how you'd like it to be.

Even though it may be difficult for you to do this with any precision right now, you'll have an approximate idea of how your life is structured and an approximate idea of how you'd like it to be. That's all we're concerned with at this stage: approximations.

The first part of what follows relates to today. It involves a few simple questionnaires and a few minutes of introspection. Then you'll be able to produce a neat little chart that sums up your habits, responsibilities, personality, occupation, and family status.

The second part relates to how you'd like your life balance to be. Bearing in mind that there are many new discoveries you're going to make in the pages ahead, whatever conclusions you reach in this section are likely to be modified or enhanced as you progress. For the moment, though, this will help crystallize how you'd eventually like your life to look.

The first step is to take a reading of the main categories that influence your life: Physical, Spiritual, Work, and Social.

A note of caution: The following mini-questionnaires are meant to be illustrative, not definitive. They should give you an impression of the underlying issues in your life, not make a judgment on them. So please don't use them to measure your status or performance against any imagined benchmark. Because there are no benchmarks! What is imbalanced for one person may be harmonious for another.

The life balance review

Place a value alongside each statement as it applies to your life. The range of responses is between "Agree strongly" and "Disagree strongly."

Agree strongly	Agree	Agree mildly	Disagree mildly	Disagree	Disagree strongly
5	4	3	2	1	0

PHYSICAL	5	4	3	2	1	0
1. I exercise regularly.						
2. I watch my diet, choosing healthy foods in preference to all others.						
3. I have no smoking or alcohol habits.						
4. I get regular, high-quality sleep.						
5. I regularly pursue recreational interests.						
Total						

SPIRITUAL	5	4	3	2	1	0
1. My life has meaning and values, and I live by these values.						
2. I find time to relax and appreciate things of artistic or natural beauty.						
3. I am growing as an individual, continually learning new things, and I have time to do this.						
4. I have meaningful life goals other than financial or work-related ones.						
5. I set aside time for myself and my reflections at least once a day.						
Total						

WORK	5	4	3	2	1	0
1. I am recognized and respected for what I do in life.						
2. I seldom take home work stresses or frustrations.						
3. I seldom feel tired because of the pressure of my job.						
4. My job is satisfying and fulfilling.						
5. At the end of each day I feel I've accomplished most of what I set out to do.						
Total						

SOCIAL	5	4	3	2	1	0
1. I have all the time I need to be with my family.						
2. I have a rich, meaningful life outside work.						
3. My work has no negative side effects in my personal life.						
4. I have a wide circle of friends and regularly spend time with them.						
5. I enjoy many fulfilling activities with my children, partner, friends, and acquaintances.						
Total						

If you total the count on each questionnaire, you'll have a reasonable idea of where the emphasis lies in the different areas of your life.

Make a note of each of these totals. Higher is better. In fact, if all four were more or less equal, that would be "perfect." It would also be unusual.

Whether your count is high or low, it's no reason to get excited— or alarmed. The purpose of these questionnaires is to determine the *spread* of your needs and influences. In themselves they mean very little. Besides, the results will probably tend toward the side of the positive because the questions are framed this way.

As long as you have four numbers in front of you, that's it for this part of the exercise.

Seeing your life balance—as it is

Now we're going to use those four numbers in a creative, intuitive way to help clarify where your life stands today. When you've completed this section, you'll have a chart that sums up what your life balance *looks* like now.

- First, photocopy or redraw the "Life balance" chart from page 237. Make a few copies of it, and keep them handy as you read through these pages.
- Assuming you've completed the questionnaires, you'll now have four numbers in front of you. We'll start with those from "Work" and "Social."
- Shade a small section of the line that joins Work and Social to show where your life is focused at this point. If, for example, your Work score is 6 and your Social score is 1, you'll shade this more toward "Work." There's no need for great accuracy here—approximate will be fine.

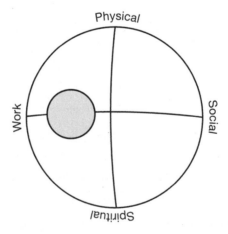

- Now, with a different colored pencil, shade the line that joins Physical and Spiritual. Say your Physical score is 18 and your

Spiritual score is 4, the part of the chart you shade will be more toward "Physical."

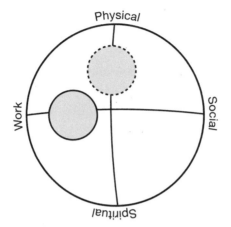

- Your chart now shows where your present life focus is. And that's it for the first part of the exercise.

What if both sets of numbers are equal and both shaded areas fall in exactly the same place? This would indicate a perfectly balanced state for some people, although each person is different. However, considering that you saw the need to read a book called *Perfect Balance*, this will probably be unlikely. Most charts I see are skewed one way or another.

Of course, it doesn't have to be like this. Whether you're a politician or a priest, a professional athlete or a homemaker, the most satisfying and rewarding approach is the well-balanced one—an evenly distributed spread of Physical, Spiritual, Work, and Social interests and activities. This is what we will work toward in the chapters ahead.

So, as approximate as it is, this chart represents the big-picture view of your life balance at this moment. This is your starting point.

You can use it as a benchmark for the changes you'll introduce as you move toward perfect balance.

Now we're going to take a big-picture glimpse of your life balance *as you'd like it to be*.

The theoretical ideal would be a harmonious, seamless spread in the center of all four coordinates (page 27). But who is a theoretical human being? I'm not. Nor are you. The ideal graph for me may skew to the right, while yours may skew to the left. In all cases, our idea of perfect balance is influenced by our particular needs, history, relationships, state of life, circumstances, and so on. What's important is that you determine the spread that works for you.

Unfortunately, you can't do this with a questionnaire. You can't even do it with logic and reason. Because, at this stage, your end point is only fantasy; it exists only in your imagination. To bring it to life, you need big-picture–forming techniques.

Big-picture–forming techniques

First, a word about logic. When your life is out of balance, it doesn't take long for you to realize that neither willpower nor analysis is going to get you out of this state in a hurry. Sooner or later you're going to have to call on your emotions and instincts as well.

The Calm Way: The less you know to be "true," the more possibilities exist.

Sometimes this requires a change in thinking style. Especially in the workplace—dominated by a logical, analytical style known as "businesslike thinking"—and when you feel pressured.

When you rely too much on analytical thinking at the expense of your intuition and emotion, you limit your mental potential. First, because you're using only part of your brainpower, and second, because you're putting barriers between yourself and your unconscious resources.

It is your subconscious mind—not your conscious mind—that will help you find the most relevant way to perfect balance. It is a vast reservoir of memory, information, knowledge, and wisdom; and it contains most of the insights and observations that you thought you'd forgotten ages ago. The only sure way to access your subconscious is by relaxing and trusting your emotions and intuition.

How to broaden your perspective

All too often the difference between success and failure, progress and regress, happiness and depression—and, yes, balance and imbalance—is simply a matter of perspective.

For example, the pattern of progress is often characterized by a couple of steps forward followed by one step backward. If your perspective is broad enough, you'll see progress in this, and the occasional setback will be something to take in your stride. On the other hand, if your perspective is narrow and too focused on detail, you'll be discouraged by that one backward step.

The same applies to introducing balance into your life. The broader your perspective, the easier it is to achieve. And if you're going to achieve *perfect* balance, you'll need to see how all the many interests and influences in your life work comfortably and harmoniously together.

Taking this holistic view is more than just a philosophical decision. It requires psychological or even physiological methods. Some of those we've developed include:

- a specific way you use your body
- the way you look at time
- the way you use your brain.

The way you use your body

Generally, the more tense you are, the more narrow your focus. When you're up against a deadline and things are going wrong, the ticking of a clock can drive you mad. Or when you're rushing to complete a balance sheet that will be rounded to the nearest dollar, you become obsessed with a column of figures that are a few cents out.

In short, you just cannot see the big picture.

Things are different when you're relaxed. Now your focus relaxes as well. Now you don't notice the ticking clock because you're aware of an entire room. Now you're not worrying about a few stray cents on the balance sheet because that is a detail for one of your team members in the days ahead.

Just by allowing your body to relax, you begin to increase your ability to see the big picture.

So maybe you can allow yourself to relax now. Just a little.

The way you look at time

When you're dealing with a big-picture topic like Your Life and trying to make accurate decisions in relation to it, you often get bogged down or sidetracked by the detail of today or this week. This narrowness will be even more pronounced if you believe you're affected by "time pressure" in one form or another.

Ironically, time pressure is seldom the result of what's actually happening at this moment. It relates more to what has already happened or what you believe may happen. In other words, your perceptions are formed by what you've already experienced (past) or what you think you're going to experience (future), rather than by what you are actually experiencing (the present).

To form a holistic view of your life, you have to see beyond the detail. The best way to do this is to relax and focus on the present.

When your mind is still and you cease to analyze or think about what you're experiencing, your focus automatically changes. You are totally aware of this moment. Without trying, you are no longer distracted by what has been happening or what may happen. Only what is happening. Without trying, you suddenly see through the clutter.

Following are two simple ways to do this. Depending on whether you're more visually oriented or feelings oriented, one will seem more natural to you.

THE FEELINGS-ORIENTED APPROACH. This is the "Calm Way to feel centered" technique in the Your Tools section on page 238. It's a 90-second thought experiment that will help you get an inkling of what it's like to feel centered and relaxed. By putting it to work now you will find it easy to discover an orderly, centered state that naturally lends itself to a more holistic perception.

THE VISUALLY ORIENTED APPROACH. If you are more visually oriented, the "Time line" approach in the Your Tools section on page 240 will help you divorce yourself from the past and future and bring your attention into the present.

Either of these exercises should be performed as preparation for others that follow. Why don't you pause for a few minutes and experiment with both?

The way you use your brain

Once you are relaxed, centered, and focused on "now," rather than thinking about the future or the past, your perspective automatically begins to widen. You can make it wider still by taking one more step, "The big-picture solution." This is covered in detail on page 241. You may like to take a look at it now, because we'll be referring to it in the next stage.

> The Calm Way: Take the time to determine where you want to end up. Because if you don't know where you're headed, no road is the right road.

Your life balance—as you want it to be

A few pages back you produced a chart that was a big-picture view of your life balance as you see it now. This was your starting point. Now you're going to create one that shows your state of life balance *as you'd like it to be*. From a general point of view, how would your life look? Which aspects of it would you play down? Which would you emphasize?

Unlike with the first chart, this one does not involve a questionnaire or any sort of brainpower. Just a few scribbles, off the top of your head, using "The big-picture solution" (page 241).

Your starting point is this: "All things being equal, what would my ideal life balance look like? How would it rearrange the Physical, Social, Spiritual, and Work emphases of my life?"

This will help you create a broad map of where you should head. It won't be specific, and it may even be superficial at this stage, but it will give you the strongest indication yet of the direction that the "inner you" would like to take in finding perfect balance. Take all the time you need; this is important. Follow these steps.

1. Make a clean copy of the "Life balance" chart (page 237).
2. Relax. Kick off your shoes and give yourself permission to take it easy for the next 15 minutes or so.
3. If it helps, follow the steps from "The big-picture solution."
4. Without analyzing in any way, highlight the parts of the chart where you feel your energies would be focused if your life was better balanced than it is now.
5. Don't be tempted to go straight to the midpoint of each line. Just shade it in a way that would make you feel more content than you are now. Depending on your likes and circumstances, it might look something like the following.

There you have it—this second chart is your destination. It's generalized, subject to revision, and completely lacking in detail. But the groundwork is now complete.

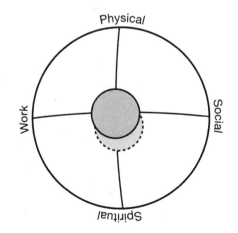

Now and when

You now have two charts: one produced logically, the other produced intuitively. The former is a holistic picture of where your life balance is now, the latter a holistic picture of how you'd like it to be.

Both charts are broad and approximate. This is exactly how they're meant to be. In the pages ahead, you will make many new discoveries that may cause you to want to modify or enhance them.

If you place these two charts side by side, you have a broad plan of

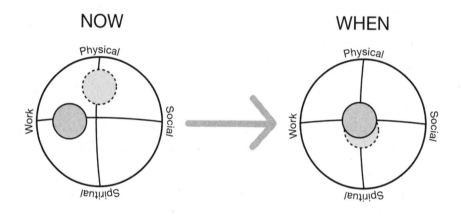

the transition you intend to make over the course of this book. This transition from "Now" to "When," or the process that is involved, is where you'll get your first taste of perfect balance.

The Calm Way: If you know where you are now and where you want to end up, perfect balance is the process in between.

How to find perfect balance

Perfect balance is usually more a state of mind
than a state of circumstances.

You can arrive at this state in a fairly linear way,
working through a variety of strategic, physical, and
psychological steps. That's what this part
of the book is about.

On the other hand, it's possible that you will arrive
here intuitively, leapfrogging many of these steps and
simply adopting the state of mind without effort.

Whatever route you take to get here, your life is in
perfect balance the moment that you feel it is.

4.

It's closer than
you thought

Perfect balance may be closer than you suspected.

In the previous chapter you produced two big-picture charts. If you take the first (your life balance as it is now) and place it alongside the second (your life as you'd like it to be), you have a guide to where you're headed. However, this is like looking at a postcard of the destination rather than a map of how to get there.

This part of the book is about creating the map. It involves four simple phases.

1. Take the first step.
2. Complete today's picture.
3. Find your center of balance.
4. Adjust.

We will cover this in much greater detail ahead, but in essence these four phases are as follows.

Take the first step

Before you begin a project, the first thing you normally do is inspect the tools or source material you have to work with. In this particular project, what you have to work with is . . . you.

As you stand now, are you capable of getting your life into balance? Is everything so organized and together in your head that, provided the right solutions are presented, you will be able to put them to immediate use? And, assuming that the remainder of this book is filled with brilliant strategies for managing your time and resources to achieve this sought-after goal, do you have the drive and energy to be able to do it?

Your inclination will be to say yes. But the more you think about it, the less certain you become. That is why the first step toward achieving perfect balance is preparation, getting your source material into shape. So, to ensure there are no obstacles on your path, the ideal starting point will involve:

- a balanced body
- a balanced mind
- a balanced spirit.

Complete today's picture

In the previous chapter, you produced a holistic view of what your life balance looks like today. You did that with very little forethought or self-examination.

This is the phase that completes that picture.

From a strategic point of view, this is the most important phase of establishing perfect balance. It's about knowing *precisely* where you are now, so that you can plan *precisely* where you'd like to be.

Being precise is no easy task. If you're like most people, your attention will be occupied by the interests and issues that are causing you problems today. This makes it difficult to see more subtle but equally powerful influences.

For example, if your partner is threatening to leave you because you're spending too much time at work and not enough with your family, you'll believe your life interests extend no further than work and home. Yet, almost certainly you have more interests and responsibilities than these two. And when you do identify them, you find that they tend to compete for your attention, often pulling in wildly different directions.

Adding to this confusion, you may feel you're expected to satisfy your own needs and expectations as well as those of your family, employer, friends, acquaintances, community, and society at large.

Perfect balance is achieved when you feel you can cater for all of the above, seamlessly and harmoniously. But before you can do that, you'll need a big-picture view of what these influences are.

> The Calm Way: Sometimes the best results are achieved not by increasing efforts but by reducing them. Strain less; achieve more.

Find your center of balance

If you've already tried the little thought experiment "The Calm Way to feel centered" on page 238, you may have experienced a subtle sensation of feeling centered and relaxed. Easy, wasn't it? If nothing much happened, don't give it another thought; I did say it was subtle. However, these sorts of experiences have a habit of creeping up on you. After working your way through this book, you may look back on this page and see that I was right, that the feeling does build as you progress.

Just for a moment we're going to move from that simple feeling into an area that looks more complicated but isn't. It's about "complex systems."

A complex system is something that's made up of several simpler components that work together as one. You find them in all areas of life: biology (people, cells, plants), ecology (weather, ozone layer), sociology (industries, nations), psychology (feelings, habits, behaviors), and even man-made systems such as computers, airplanes, and corporations.

For a complex system to perform the way it's supposed to, it needs to achieve and maintain equilibrium—a perfect balance among all its components. To manage this it constantly makes tiny adjustments that compensate for environmental changes or unforeseen disturbances. As a result, it is always moving between stability and instability, always in a state of minor adjustment. This is called "homeostasis."

The complex system you are most familiar with is your body. It's made up of many components, some of which may even be described as complex systems in their own right. Your central nervous system is one of these.

One function of your central nervous system is to control body temperature. The body's ideal core temperature is 98.6°F. This is what we call your temperature control's "balance point."

When the outside temperature changes, which it does constantly throughout the day, your body has to compensate; it brings into play a range of biological functions that rebalance your system so this ideal temperature can be maintained. Sometimes this is not sufficient, and you have to intervene. For example, if the outside temperature drops too much, you might need a blanket. Or if illness causes your body temperature to rise, you might need medicine. Because if equilibrium is not restored, nasty things occur.

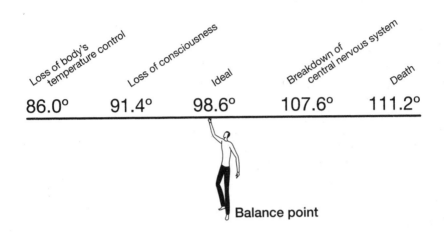

Whether the complex system in question is your central nervous system, your emotions, a weather system, or a commercial organization, the principle remains the same: to survive and thrive, balance has to be maintained.

Your balance point

What if you could identify a point, as unambiguous as your ideal body temperature, that could act as the fulcrum for your life's efforts and concerns? Not only would this make it easier to find balance in the first place, but it would provide a benchmark you could refer to whenever the need arose. Then, as your world evolved, as unplanned events came and went, as various influences grew or diminished in importance, you'd always know how to maintain direction and purpose in your life.

Soon you're going to create a balance point for yourself. We call this your center of balance. It will help you establish and maintain a calm, orderly state of perfect balance. It will also act as a way to help you recover from disappointments and setbacks.

As you know only too well, it's comparatively easy to feel calm and in control when your life is running smoothly and everything is in place. It's easy to feel focused and energetic after you've just returned to work after a restful vacation. It's easy to be attentive and understanding when you're enjoying a pleasant day with your family.

But when the pressure grows, the unexpected happens, or something goes wrong with your plans, how do you feel? Suddenly the vacation or family outing you've just returned from is the furthest thing from your mind. You try to hang on to the feeling or to bring it back in some way, but it just doesn't happen for you anymore. All that rest and conviviality, all that reservoir of energy and tolerance—where's it all gone? How did it vanish so quickly?

Having a well-defined center of balance will help you to continue feeling centered and in control no matter what is going on around you.

Adjust

Once you have a clear view of how your life looks now and how you'd like it to be in the future, it simply becomes a matter of massaging or rearranging the various elements so that the balance shifts from "here" to "there." Your center of balance is the point that you realign them around.

And it's the point that you *continue* to align them around.

As your life is a "complex system," it requires continual fine adjustments if it is to maintain equilibrium. Why? Because the world is ever-changing. Circumstances change. Economies change. Regulations change. Employers change. Your work, family, and acquaintances change. So it follows that from time to time you might have to change a little yourself. The pages ahead are crammed with strategies and techniques that will help you do this in a relaxed and orderly fashion.

The Four Phases to Perfect Balance

1. **Take the first step.** This is the preparation phrase, where you inspect and hone the source material you have to work with—your body, mind, and spirit.

2. **Complete today's picture.** Before you go too far, you need a clear idea of your needs, roles, and responsibilities—the detail of your state of life balance as it is *now*.

3. **Find your center of balance.** You determine where your ideal balance point should be, with a view to rearranging the various influences of your life around it. This is how you'd like your life to be balanced *in the future*.

4. **Adjust.** You make adjustments to the weighting of your life pressures and influences to bring them into line with your ideal of perfect balance. You continue to make small adjustments as life moves on.

5.

PHASE I:
Take the first step

When you try to walk a balance beam for the first time, or ride a skateboard, or stand on one leg while tying a shoelace, you make a discovery about the physical nature of balance.

- If you're fit and healthy, balance is easier.
- If your mind is still and free from anxiety, balance is easier.
- If you have an untroubled and optimistic outlook, balance is easier.

In other words, if you start out with an evenly balanced body, mind, and spirit, any form of balance is easier to achieve. Then, if you want to improve that balance even further, it becomes a simple matter of practice and fine-tuning.

In a physical sense this is fairly easy to grasp. You've probably experienced it at one time or another.

When you explore further, you discover that the same body-mind-spirit principle applies in the arts, sports, martial arts, business performance, therapy, and so on. So the obvious question that arises is: "If my body, mind, and spirit were in balance, wouldn't it follow that the rest of my life would start to feel more balanced as well?"

Unquestionably yes. But while "more balanced" is a worthwhile ideal, it might be a long way from perfect balance. Perfect balance requires *every* aspect of your life to feel integrated and whole—body, mind, spirit, work, family, ambitions, recreation—the lot.

> The Calm Way: When you feel perfectly centered,
> your mind, body, and spirit work as one.

Establishing this balance of body, mind, and spirit has many life-enriching benefits, not the least of which is that you'll feel like a more powerful being. You'll be able to confidently say, no matter what's going on around you, "I feel centered and in control."

From where you're sitting now, does that seem like a big task? There you are, swamped with responsibilities, craving a bit more freedom and evenness in your life, and I'm urging you to take on yet another responsibility: getting your body, mind, and spirit into balance. How does that make you feel?

If you were to approach this in the conventional way (the hard way), it would seem like a daunting task. But the Calm Way is a breeze. Not only is it easy to understand and implement, but it should also be enjoyable.

First, there are two work issues that may have to be dealt with: embedded tension and burnout. If they're part of your life, they'll get in the way of your progress. So let's deal with them right away.

Embedded tension

"Embedded tension" is a term we coined to describe the stress and strain that stems from one part of your life—usually work—being carried over into other parts of your life.

We single out this particular problem because it is rampant in today's fast-moving world, and if left unresolved, it can undermine your efforts to find perfect balance.

Embedded tension is what some people refer to as stress. However, it's not just on-the-job stress, which to some extent is inevitable, but take-home stress as well. It makes it difficult for you to relax and focus on any activity that occurs outside your occupation. It limits your capacity to enjoy life, particularly those parts of it that don't have a productivity component. It reduces your self-esteem and makes you feel more negative. And it's often hard to recognize because it desensitizes you to the impact stress has on your behavior and on the feelings of those around you.

The overriding characteristic of embedded tension is that you can't leave the stress of your normal day at work. No matter how hard you try, no matter what you do to distract yourself when you go home in the evening, the pressure lingers in the background. It wearies you and shortens your temper. It numbs you to the appeal and attractions of people and other sides of life. It drives you to slavishly watch television or read the paper, not for entertainment or enlightenment but for the refuge they provide. Not only is this kind of emotional withdrawal unhealthy for the individual, but it can also be a big strain on relationships.

The causes of embedded tension include all of those you associate with workplace stress, such as management practices, change, physical environment, and so on. The most common offenders are time, control, relationships, and choice of job.

Time

Whenever we do a survey about how people feel about workplace stress, one word invariably tops the list: time. Or lack thereof. As the world gets busier and more compressed, as the demands of your work and social connections increase rather than diminish, you discover it's the one aspect of life you have least control over.

The Calm Way to regain some of that control is to use "The moment is now" method on page 243. Try it the next time you're feeling under pressure.

There's another side to time pressure. It relates to things that are not happening, have never happened, and probably never will. Worry, fear, and anxiety, for example, create such time pressures. They are always future-based, and they relate to events or possibilities that seldom eventuate. See "Putting worries in their place" in the Your Tools section on page 245.

Control

The less control you believe you exert over the important areas of your life—career, job, health, relationships—the more likely you are to suffer a degree of stress in relation to them.

This is why you feel stressed and frustrated when you have to perform monotonous, repetitive tasks. Or when you feel you lack choices in any particular situation. Sometimes even when you feel you have too many choices.

In a work environment, this not just the result of lowly positions with demanding supervisors. It can also be the product of doubt and insecurity arising from being promoted beyond your capabilities. Or if you are in a new position and haven't yet grasped all that's involved. Or from being unsure where to focus your efforts because your boss has planned poorly or not provided a thorough job definition.

Whenever you feel you have no control over a situation, you begin to feel that it is in control of you rather than the other way around—a recipe for feeling tense and pressured.

Once again, check out "The moment is now" on page 243. It's a powerful way to feel more in control of the tasks and expectations of your immediate world.

> The Calm Way: When you focus totally on the activity before you—however mundane it may appear—you feel more in control of what you do, and you get more satisfaction from your efforts.

Relationships

You will not be surprised to read that relationships can be one of the major sources of pressure in the workplace. Yet the more obvious causes of relationship strain—such as personal conflicts, lack of respect, envy, unfair comparison, and competition—will not usually be the main pressure in your work life.

Overwhelmingly, this will come from those you work closely with. In other words, peer pressure. Even more persistent and intrusive than the expectations of a demanding boss are the expectations of your colleagues. If the rest of the team works past 7 p.m., you will feel obliged to work similarly. If the rest of the team takes work home every night, there will be pressure on you to do so as well.

And, ironically, it is usually easier to moderate the expectations of your boss than it is to influence the behavior of a team.

Choice of job

If you're in a role you don't like, or that bothers you, or that offends your principles in some way, the chances are it will become an ongoing source of tension and aggravation. The more senior your position, the more aggravating this will become.

The seriousness of this predicament is often overlooked. Yet there's ample evidence to show that the emotional fallout from being in a job you dislike gets worse over time. Left unchecked, it can lead to burnout.

"Just walk away," some might say. This is not always appropriate. If you're under contract, or have no suitable alternative in mind, or if you've invested many years in a role, or you love particular aspects of your job, changing might be the last thing you want to do. In many ways it can be like being trapped in an unsatisfying relationship—extracting yourself from it can be more stressful than actually being in it.

> The Calm Way: Half the enjoyment of your job is simply making the decision to enjoy it.

The key to knowing which way to turn is determining what's important in your life. Once you have a clear idea of what your priorities are, it's amazing how quickly other facets of your life—such as your choice of job—fall into place. Then, when you evaluate the appropriateness of the role you're in, you just have to ask three simple questions.

- Does it support or is it linked to my life priorities?
- Does it clash with them?
- Is it irrelevant to them?

Your course of action depends on your answer. If your job supports or is linked to your priorities, you probably need to find another way of dealing with your frustrations. An excellent way is "A stretch of the imagination" on page 246, or "A change of perspective" on page 248.

If your job or position clashes with your priorities or offends your values in some way, you should probably consider a change. There are obvious steps to be taken here. See "The big decision" on page 250.

If your job or position is irrelevant to your life's priorities, you're still faced with the choice of changing jobs or improving your current one, but at least you will feel free to move either way.

Of course, all of the above presupposes that you know what your priorities are. Most people believe they have numerous priorities, and most believe that it is not only possible but essential to manage these simultaneously. Yet the more priorities you believe you have, the more pressure you will feel.

When you have your priorities in order, you'll find it easy to see through the distractions, to focus on what will serve you best, and to effectively deal with the big decisions. Determining your values and priorities is covered in greater detail later.

Burnout

Although widely spoken about, burnout is one of the least recognized and understood by-products of work stress. It is a form of physical, emotional, and mental exhaustion that many experience at some time or another in their careers. Just like midlife crisis, there are all sorts of theories about why it occurs and how it should be handled, but the ones I subscribe to are the commonsense ones.

Burnout usually occurs in highly motivated people who have high expectations of success. They begin full of energy and enthusiasm and are extremely positive about what lies ahead. Then the change begins. Their rosy view of what was possible starts to fade. Their original expectations now look unrealistic; nothing seems to be happening the way they planned. Where are the results? Where's the recognition? They put even more effort into correcting this state of affairs—working harder, longer. To no end. Confusion sets in. They're tired. Frustrated. Disillusioned. Negative. Bored. The driven, energetic go-getter has become lethargic and irritable. "Is it that I'm incompetent or a failure?" they wonder.

In this early phase, burnout candidates find it increasingly difficult to apply themselves and to concentrate. They find themselves going over the same things, almost compulsively, and usually not to any great effect. They become indecisive. They are vulnerable to colds and illness. Their motivation goes out the window. Without ever really noticing the change taking place, they suddenly find that all they're doing is going through the motions, without getting any satisfaction or stimulation. Sometimes it's hard to even go through the motions.

If you intervene at these early stages, burnout is relatively easy to reverse. Left unattended, it can deteriorate. Then the overriding characteristic becomes despair—"I'm a failure," "I can't go on with this," "I'm just going to quit and take off somewhere." Depression creeps in. And it can go even further, leading to physical or mental breakdown.

Not surprisingly, some of the causes of burnout include those we've already addressed—time, control, and choice. The main ones, though, relate to drive and ambition. When you have unrealistically high ambitions or goals, or when a job or task involves a great deal of effort and conscientiousness but shows no obvious result, you are at most risk. This is why burnout is especially common in sports and management.

Overcoming the effects of burnout

There are some who believe that burnout in the workplace is purely the result of an adverse job situation and therefore cannot be remedied through personal change or improvement.

I dispute this. If we recognize the presence of burnout early enough and take steps to correct it before it becomes too advanced, it's comparatively easy to manage. In advanced cases it may require professional intervention, but it certainly can be helped—if not completely reversed—through a combination of patience, balance, modified goals, rest, and relaxation—supplemented, of course, by the skills and strategies in the pages ahead.

If you believe you are a potential victim of burnout, you can prevent it making too great an impact by doing the following:

- Cut yourself some slack. Make a practice of taking time off—a whole day is ideal—to examine your goals and priorities. Be prepared to lower your benchmarks and extend your time frames. Modify your goals as necessary, and rank them in order of priority.

  Consider the demands made on you by other people. If these

are excessive, unrealistic, unfair, or in conflict with your own goals and priorities, turn them down.

- Take up an involving but nonoccupational interest, hobby, or sport. Immerse yourself in it.
- Above all, start a healthy mind-body-spirit program. Make sure you have adequate rest, a balanced diet, and regular exercise. Limit your consumption of alcohol and caffeine.

From a work point of view, there are five steps that will make a difference almost immediately.

- Have an unambiguous idea of where you want to end up. This is different from setting goals; it's having a clear, mental picture of yourself once you have achieved the balanced life you crave. (See "Go forward, step back" on page 252.)
- Do one thing at a time. Forget about multitasking and how many things you have to achieve within a certain time frame. Concentrate on doing one thing at a time, to the best of your ability and with absolute dedication.
- Allow yourself to succeed. Burnout is often caused when there is a disconnection between ambition and ability or feasibility. It can be avoided as long as you have some degree of success. Make some of your targets and goals smaller so that you're sure to reach them, and don't forget to reward yourself when you do.
- Love what you do. If you can't be in the job you love, learn to love the job you're in. The same advice applies to occupations.
- Redefine your job. If things are serious and you can't see any way out of it, bite the bullet and change jobs. (First weigh it up with "The big decision" technique on page 250.) Or take a new position with the same employer. If this cannot be done, redefine what your job means to you. Find a new way of looking at it. A couple of the more successful ways are the psychological techniques you'll find

in the Your Tools section—"A change of perspective" on page 248 or "A stretch of the imagination" on page 246.

It's important to remember that burnout is not a clear-cut ailment like tonsillitis. There are many shades, and it affects different people to greater and lesser degrees. Most important, it begins and ends in your mind. By adopting the appropriate attitude, being focused, and ensuring that you are physically healthy and strong, you can overcome it. You *can* overcome it; you have already begun.

(In extreme cases, or if in doubt, consult a health professional.)

Balancing mind, body, and spirit

Now that we have a greater understanding of burnout and embedded tension, and know how to deal with them, it's time to move on to the fun part—getting your mind, body, and spirit into shape.

In this section we're going to cover a range of topics such as diet, exercise, and getting proper rest. You may be wondering why you'd want to read about diet and exercise when all you want to know is how to find more hours in the day. But, as you'll soon see, they are related; in fact, they are the foundations of your life of perfect balance.

> The Calm Way: When it comes to how balanced you feel
> your life is, regular exercise and a healthy diet are every
> bit as important as your work and your workload.

Trying to establish balance in one part of your life without taking into consideration the others is a recipe for disappointment. To put this into a more compelling framework, consider the following questions:

- What if you made your work and home into a showpiece of balance, then you were retrenched?
- What if you finally worked out how to harmonize all your work and lifestyle issues, then your partner walked out?

As bleak as they may be, these scenarios show that it takes more than a partial balance to sustain you through life's inevitable and unpredictable changes.

Perfect balance means total harmony—not just between work and private life, not just with your interests and ambitions, but with your physical health, mental health, and spiritual fulfillment. This holistic ideal recognizes that you are more than just a body and mind; you are a complex system of cells, biases, attitudes, relationships, beliefs, and states of health—all of which must harmonize within themselves, as well as with a much wider world.

To ensure that the foundation is in place, you really need to consider five different areas: exercise, diet, attitude, calm, and volunteering.

Exercise for a balanced body

Can you remember a time when exercise was a joy rather than a discipline? We used to do it for the sheer love of getting outside and having fun. What happened?

No doubt you're aware of the health and longevity benefits of regular exercise. You may also be aware of the emotional benefits. It helps you cope with a busy, complex life. It directly counters the effects of negative stress and reverses the physical processes that lead to it. It freshens your mind and lifts your mood. It calms the nerves and helps you to sleep better. It improves your state of mental health, helping you fight depression, anxiety, worry, and a whole range of emotional and psychological conditions. And of course it can work wonders in toning and shaping your body.

With so many obvious benefits, why doesn't everybody embrace regular exercise?

"Too busy." "Too boring." "Too unfit." "Novelty wore off." "I'm going to take it up in the summer." "I look awful in tights." "Can't afford a gym membership." "I have an exercise bike somewhere in the attic."

But even more common is the way people think of exercise in the same way they think of work—as another obligation to be dealt with. Maybe this explains why so many people abandon their exercise programs when they're on vacation.

The Calm Way to approach exercise seeks to reestablish the link between exercise and enjoyment.

Benchmarks—gone!

Exercise is one of life's most benchmarked activities. When it comes to aerobic exercise, for example, some books and articles are painfully specific about details such as the desired pulse rate and duration in order to achieve a *minimum* level of fitness!

If you have the motivation to pursue this, and the patience and mathematical capability to work out the specifics, go for it. In this case, the "hard way" has something to offer. But if you're an everyday person who needs to walk before you can run, then the Calm Way will have more appeal. It's a minimum-level routine you can enjoy rather than endure.

The Calm Way has no minimum performance levels or bench-marks. It says you should do the best you can manage, as regularly as possible, and have fun while you're doing it. It focuses on a combination of "incidental exercise" and "pleasure sessions," instead of gyms, personal trainers, skipping ropes, step machines, and Lycra bicycle pants—unless you have a particular fondness for these.

Incidental exercise is by far the easiest way to improve your fitness. The old belief that a regular training program was the only way has been shown to be a fallacy; you can get the same health and longevity benefits through a modest increase in your overall level of physical activity—gardening, sometimes taking the stairs rather than the elevator, doing the shopping, walking the dog, doing the housework, walking an extra block to buy your lunch, or leaving your car at the distant end of the parking lot. If all this incidental exercise adds up to an hour or even half an hour a day—which is not difficult when you consider all the different activities you participate in—you'll be in good shape.

The alterative to this is five "pleasure sessions" or mini-escapes a week—even more if you can manage it—in a more structured routine. A routine that gives you pleasure. Preferably at an intensity that warms you up and causes you to breathe more heavily than usual. You don't have to sweat or strain, but be aware of the principle that brisk is good and brisker is better. And because this is the Calm Way, you can be relaxed about the ideal of five days a week. If you achieve it 80 percent of the time—that is four of the five days in a week—you're doing well. If you miss a couple of days, or take the elevator rather than the stairs, or go less briskly than usual, you've got nothing to feel guilty about. All you've done is miss out on the pleasure it would have brought. As long as you're firing up your body on a regular basis—maybe with a view to extending the intensity and duration over time—you'll feel better about yourself.

(By the way, the experts say your pulse rate should not exceed 75 percent of your recommended maximum, and you should have a checkup before you start any exercise program—especially if you're over forty.)

> The Calm Way: Work toward 30–60 minutes of incidental exercise a day, or 4–5 "pleasure sessions" a week, where you breathe more heavily than usual. Brisk is good; brisker is better. But if you can't manage this on occasion, don't worry.

Exercise as pleasure

You know you're exercising the Calm Way when you look forward to it for the pleasure it brings rather than for the good it does. If you can rediscover the joy of being more active throughout your day, then incidental exercise may be ideal. All you have to do is look for ways to extend your pleasures throughout the day: you might discover a stroll in the park at lunchtime is more rewarding than sitting in the office, or the stairwell is more of an adventure than the crowded elevator.

If you prefer a more structured form of exercise, choose the one that gives you the most pleasure. Do you like to swim, skate, run, row, surf, cycle, skip, or dance? If you have to think about this, choose walking. Walking has an exercise benefit and a calming benefit. It doesn't require any training. You won't look untrained or awkward. No one's going to question whether you're wearing the right gear or are using the right steps. It's portable, relaxing, and second nature. You can combine it with other activities such as gardening, sightseeing, or visiting friends. And, best of all, you can do it in a *place* that gives you pleasure as well.

Now here's how to transform a simple walk into a pleasurable escape.

- First, schedule 30 minutes into each day's routine. This is a time you reserve just for yourself—your own private escape time. Unwinding time. Energizing-yourself-for-the-day time. Luxuriating-in-your-own-company time. Sure, it's a bit of an indulgence, but you deserve it. Think of it as an escape. You have no obligation other than to enjoy the experience.
- Now, apply your full attention to your walking. Concentrate on each step. Feel the soles of your feet as they touch the ground. Concentrate on maintaining good posture, on feeling loose and free. Strive to do it as thoroughly and gracefully as you can.
- If you're in a place that gives you pleasure, be aware of your surroundings. Appreciate every sight, sound, scent, temperature change, and texture. Soon you'll be totally absorbed by the activity.

A pleasure for the rest of your body

Regular exercise has other benefits. The better your muscle tone, the better you look, and the more fat you burn (around 700 calories more per month for every pound of muscle). Muscle-strengthening exercises also improve bone density, which helps reduce the chances of osteoporosis later in life.

The hard way to strengthen your muscles is by pumping weights and pushing around gym equipment. The Calm Way is to have a few mini-routines, which, as well as strengthening your muscles, amuse the pets and family during the commercial breaks on television. I've included a few simple ones here, but you'll be able to think up others.

PUSH. These mini push-ups will help strengthen your arm, chest, and shoulder muscles.

Instead of balancing on your toes and lifting your entire body weight with your arms—as with traditional push-ups—balance on your knees. This means less strain.

SIT. Some people call these stomach crunches. They help strengthen your stomach muscles, which in turn helps to diminish back problems.

Lie on the floor with your knees bent and your feet flat on the floor. Allow your back muscles to relax. Focus on contracting your stomach muscles so that you lift your shoulders a *short* distance from the floor. Slowly return to the start position.

You can make these even more entertaining by doing them on an exercise ball.

PEDAL. This is an exercise that helps strengthen your lower abdominal muscles. And, because you do it one leg at a time, it also helps your core body strength. The action is like pedaling a bicycle; it's very easy to master.

Start in the same position as for the sit-ups above. With both knees raised, slowly extend your right leg horizontally until your heel touches the floor. Slowly bring it back, then repeat with your left leg.

If you're flexible enough you can make this
even more effective by doing the following.

With your knees bent to a 45-degree
angle, slowly start "pedaling." As you
do so, touch your left elbow to your right
knee, then your right elbow to your left knee.

How many do you need to do? Groups of 10–20 repetitions of
each exercise are a good starting point. If it hurts, do fewer. If you
find it easy, do more. Whether you do one exercise or many depends
on your level of flexibility, strength, and commitment. It might also
depend on what's on television. If you were to combine these exercises with slow and leisurely stretching, you'd feel like a new person
in no time.

Clearly, the Calm Way to exercise is moderate in its scope. Unless
you push yourself, it won't bring you even close to peak fitness or
cardiovascular perfection. You probably won't end up with rippling
pectorals and biceps. Power walkers and gym junkies will zoom past
you, sweating more, frowning more, and probably with better lungs,
calves, and butts. But, hey, you'll be enjoying it more! And for you,
exercise is an escape. For them, it's a chore.

Diet for a balanced body

What you eat plays a major role in your state of health.

From the negative perspective, some estimates say more than 50
percent of diagnosed illnesses in the developed world are linked to
diet. From the positive perspective, you can improve your immune
system and overall state of health, and prevent or delay most cardiovascular diseases and other degenerative illnesses, through dietary

measures. You can also influence how you feel and how you deal with the stresses and strains of life.

Yet, mention the word "diet" to most people and they think of fat, losing weight, and going without. Clearly, there is an imbalance in the way we even think of diet.

The Calm Way to approach diet establishes a balance between wellness, appearance, and feeling. It helps you to feel energetic and alive. It focuses on health and longevity. Yet it's so flexible you'll be able to relax and enjoy it with minimal study or willpower. All through a balance in four different areas: quality, wholeness, combinations, and quantity.

QUALITY. Technically speaking, there are three main types of stresses in life: mechanical stresses, emotional stresses, and chemical stresses. A primary cause of chemical stress is the foods (which are essentially chemicals) we consume. An unbalanced diet deprives the body of essential nutrients, which causes stress on the body. Overeating leads to obesity, which places your organs under stress. And you know about the negative impacts of caffeine, preservatives, excessive alcohol, tobacco, and refined sugar.

You can avoid much of this by choosing foods that are close to the way nature intended, in terms of freshness (fresh, unpreserved), wholeness (unrefined), and simplicity of preparation (not overly cooked or overspiced).

As far as freshness is concerned, it is amazing how many people with "sophisticated" palates cannot taste the difference between one fresh vegetable and another. The difference can be profound. If your palate has been bombarded with strong flavors and dynamic seasonings, you may have lost this ability. But pay close attention to what you're eating, and you can reverse this in forty-eight hours. Then a whole new world of subtle, fresh flavors awaits.

It's not always practical to expect the best-quality foods at all times. So the Calm Way recommends that 80 percent of your food (measured by plate area) be what you'd define as "good quality." For example, if all your fruits and vegetables were high quality, you could afford to be a bit more liberal with the other 20 percent.

WHOLENESS. If you want to feel healthy and enjoy the benefits of a high-fiber diet, choose wholefoods—foods that remain as close as possible to the way they originally grew.

Foods are like machines; to function at their best, all parts need to work as one. If you pull a machine apart and throw away all the bits you don't understand or like the look of, you might end up with something that appears similar to the original but will never function the way it was meant to. Yet this is what we do with foods every day.

There is no comparison between real wholefood and reconstructed wholefood. The real one uses the complete natural product (such as a grain); the reconstructed one uses part of it. The former is a perfectly balanced food; the latter is a man-made concoction that fails to take into account all the subtleties in the food and in the human digestive system. The former features all the essential nutrients—proteins, carbohydrates, fats, and water—the way nature intended, while the latter tries to improve on this natural balance, usually with unpredictable results. (The low-fat revolution is a good example: no matter how much fat was removed from foods, people still put on weight.)

Whole*grain* foods such as brown rice, whole wheat, and oatmeal satisfy your body's needs for carbohydrates, but in a more wholesome way than refined foods such as white bread, white rice, and pasta.

Because you digest wholegrain carbohydrates much more slowly than their refined counterparts, your blood sugar levels rise at a much steadier pace—which means you are satisfied with smaller quantities, and your body handles it better. This is why wholegrains are considered to be the most important component of a well-balanced diet. (See the new food pyramid on page 102.)

I am not proposing that you get obsessive about this. There's no need to go searching for rare food products or to get into any of the exotic disciplines such as bio-organics or macrobiotics. All I'm suggesting is that you think about the food items you are about to buy—fruits, grains, vegetables, legumes—and wherever possible choose the complete food in preference to the altered one. It becomes second nature after a while. Sometimes it might pay to look a bit further than the supermarket shelves for them.

The Calm Way recognizes that an all-wholefood diet might be difficult to achieve at all times. So the balance we strive for is 80 percent wholefoods and 20 percent whatever you choose.

COMBINATIONS. Probably the most visible demonstration of balance in a dietary sense is the combinations of foods you consume. The right balance makes you feel healthy and alive; the wrong balance leaves you feeling tense and lethargic.

There was a time when we thought we knew what a well-balanced diet was. We learned about major food groups, and how the "ideal" diet should conform to certain ratios within these groups. You will recall the old food guide pyramid that influenced so many people. While it worked as a safeguard against malnutrition and satisfied a number of political needs from various grower groups, it was hardly what you'd call a sophisticated approach for an overrefined, additive-enriched, convenience-food age.

If we were to update that food guide pyramid so it took into account all of the current knowledge on dietary effects, it would look more like this:

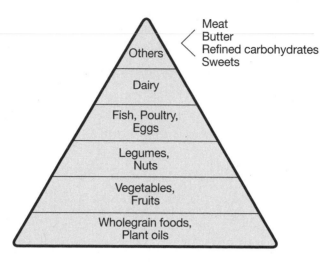

The Calm Way to balance your diet starts with this knowledge, then goes one step further.

Broadly speaking, foods can be divided into two categories: acid-forming and alkali-forming. Disproportionately more of the former can have an adverse effect on tissues and cells, as well as on the way you feel. This doesn't mean acid-forming foods are bad, just that they need to be appropriately balanced with alkali-forming foods.

Getting the balance right not only helps you feel healthier and more alive, it plays a major role in your overall state of health. It also influences your mood: alkali-forming foods tend to encourage calm, while acid-forming foods can produce unrest.

The Calm Way to approach dietary combinations is to apply a simple 80:20 formula to these two categories: 80 percent alkali-forming foods to 20 percent acid-forming foods. Rather than getting too hung up on measuring the proportions, you can think of it in terms of how much space it takes up on your plate.

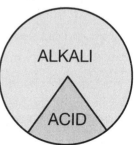

Choose from the following table.

Alkali-forming (80 percent)	Acid-forming (20 percent)
• Fresh vegetables	• All animal products—meat, fish, poultry, eggs, dairy
• Fresh fruits	• All grains—wheat, oats, flour, millet, rice
• Fresh herbs	
• Sprouted seeds	• Dried beans, seeds, nuts
• Dried fruits	• Sugar, salt, pepper, spices
• Molasses, maple syrup, cane syrup, apple cider vinegar	• Coffee, tea, fizzy drinks, alcohol
	• All processed, refined, and canned foods

There will be times when it's difficult to maintain this balance. No sweat. The Calm Way suggests that you strive toward this ideal 80 percent of the time; if you fall a bit short 20 percent of the time, relax, there's always tomorrow.

QUANTITY. You can have the best-quality wholefoods in the right combinations, yet still have an unbalanced diet if you overlook quantity.

While half of the world worries about how they can get more to eat, and the other half worries about how they can eat less, is it any wonder that the issue of food quantity is the greatest source of dietary imbalance? Whichever way you look at it, a quantity imbalance produces a range of health issues: too little food deprives you of essential nutrients, which can lead to physical and mental ailments; too much food leads to conditions that put your organs under stress.

In a world so obsessed with fad diets (most *are* fad diets), you'd think the quantity of our food consumption would play a much clearer role in our consciousness than it does. Let's see if we can make it a bit clearer. . . .

The Calm Way to approach quantity in your diet follows a very simple formula: intake is balanced by expenditure. The level of food (calories) you consume is balanced by the level of energy (calories) you expend.

intake   **exercise**

If you consume disproportionately more than you expend, you affect your health and waistline. If you consume too little, you end up malnourished. The question is how much is too much, and how much is too little?

Broadly speaking, the developed world diet skews toward too much. That's a good starting point. (If you have any form of illness or eating disorder, it may *not* be a good starting point. Better get some professional advice first.) But how much is too much? Fortunately, there's no mystery here because all kinds of guides are available—common sense, keeping a record of calories, or even calculating Weight Watchers points if you have access to them. The key here is to get a feel for the appropriate portion sizes and then to stick to those sizes.

Or get smaller plates.

While we're on the topic of quantity, let's take a brief look at the most interest-worthy aspect of this: weight control. There is no shortage of fad diets that claim to be effective. But these are far removed from a balanced diet and have little to recommend them in the longer term. So what is the secret to keeping your weight in order? For a start, foods affect people in different ways. Broadly speaking, though, it's exactly what you've known all along: choose good fresh foods, avoid too many of the obviously fattening ones, and *gradually* adjust the balance and portions. Include a greater proportion of wholefoods and you'll find their high-fiber content makes them more satisfying, which means you need smaller quantities to feel satisfied. Keep to the 80:20 formula of food combinations, and you're on easy street.

Oh, don't forget the most important step: Stick with it!

The Calm Way to manage all of the above is to determine the ideal portion sizes for you according to the amount of energy you expend and then to stick to these sizes 80 percent of the time. If you miss out on this ideal on 20 percent of occasions—that's about four meals a week—you're still doing okay.

Attitude for a balanced mind

One of the first things we learn in life is that it's easier to complain about what's wrong than it is to offer a solution. Fittingly, the person who makes the observation is usually the one who derives the most misery, because by focusing on what's wrong or bad, they are the most burdened by it. Even the most subtle negative thoughts can upset the flow of your day and lead to you feeling pressured and less able to cope.

Conversely, there are so many rewards that come from looking for constructive possibilities and the good in life, that you'd be crazy to pass them up when they're offered.

And they're always offered!

Cynics sometimes point to a distinction between optimists and "realists"—as if they were alternatives—with the implication being that realists have a better fix on reality than their happier counterparts. But an optimist is just someone who looks forward to life getting better. (Consider the alternative!) Your view of life need not be a fixture; it's a choice. You can look for the seamy side of it or you can look for the beauty; they're both there. You also have a choice in the approach you take: you can choose to pursue it positively and creatively or you can be narrow and defensive.

Why choose the positive? A positive approach outperforms the negative in almost every respect. Positive language communicates more effectively than negative. Positive instructions are more persuasive than negative. Positive goals are easier to attain than negative ones.

But far more important, a positive or optimistic outlook is guaranteed to make your life happier and more balanced. It lifts the mood and helps overcome depression and anxiety. It has a direct and measurable link with health and longevity. It plays a key role in achievement. It produces strength and perseverance. It even reduces the incidence of accidents or "bad luck" (true, there are statistics that prove it).

So, is this all just wishful thinking on my part, or can you really just switch on a positive attitude when needed?

Naturally positive

It is true that some people are more inclined toward having a positive attitude than others. But whatever your natural disposition, you can easily adopt a more positive approach. What's more, if you do it the Calm Way, you'll enjoy doing so.

While most people think they have a fair idea of whether they have a positive or negative approach to life, their assessment is often way off the mark—especially if they're driven, achievement-oriented, or overwhelmed by work. Considering that most people are a poor judge of their own attitudes and behavior, it may pay to check how you relate to the following propositions.

My approach	Always	Some-times	Never
• I am "for" rather than "against" most things.			
• I can't wait to get into my work or play in the morning.			
• When opportunities arise, I readily respond to them.			
• When difficulties or challenges arise, I readily face them.			
• I readily accept responsibility.			
• I have all the energy I need to respond to whatever arises.			
• I can stay interested in my work or other activities for extended periods.			
• I am untroubled by other people's success in my area.			
• I am more interested in what's ahead or what's happening now than what's happened before.			
Total			

The more times you answer "Always" to the above, the more positive and optimistic your approach is. Having such an outlook usually means you have the enthusiasm to succeed in what you do and enjoy it while doing so.

On the other hand, having lots of "Never's" means you will profit by implementing some of the steps that follow.

The Calm Way to feel positive and optimistic

You'll agree that having a positive approach to life is more desirable than the alternative. Desiring is the easy part; achieving it may take more effort. But, as with most improvements in life, there's a hard way to approach it, and there's the Calm Way.

The hard way attempts to do this by banishing negative thinking through willpower. The problem is that willpower has very little influence over the way you think or feel; psychologically speaking, you can't consciously force yourself *not* to think in a certain way.

The Calm Way is the opposite of this. Instead of trying to dispel negatives, it instills positives. And it does this through physiological, philosophical, and psychological approaches.

The **PHYSIOLOGICAL** approach is already second nature to you. It's something you've been doing instinctively since the earliest age.

Try it now: Smile. Go on—feel the corners of your mouth turning up. A little more now, until you can feel the corners of your eyes begin to wrinkle.

This simple act of turning up the corners of the mouth into a smile not only relaxes your facial muscles but stimulates the pleasure centers of your brain. This causes a range of neurochemicals to be produced, which trigger a range of physiological events that relate to how you feel. So a smile automatically translates into a feeling of happiness and optimism, whether this was your intention or not. Moreover, it does it without any overt effort on your part.

This is easy to accept. You've spent a lifetime training yourself to associate smiling with pleasure and feeling good. So when you do it now, you are bringing back all those positive associations.

You can make this experience even more powerful by holding your head high and moving a bit more enthusiastically than you would normally do.

The **PHILOSOPHICAL** approach is straightforward but often overlooked.

- Make up your mind to see the uplifting side of life. Choose to focus on the good and positive, and you'll soon be feeling that way yourself. Guaranteed.
- Make an effort to be "for" things, rather than "against" them. Avoid complaining; it takes a lot of energy and it's always focused on what's wrong rather than what's right.
- Go easy on your imperfections. They're what make you who you are.
- Disregard all norms and comparisons. Set your own standards.
- Feel free to do what you want and what you enjoy. Try to enjoy the small and simple things.
- Mix with positive people. Do what you can for those less fortunate than yourself.
- Enjoy the journey.

The **PSYCHOLOGICAL** approach can be even more powerful.

It boils down to understanding two things: first, having a positive outlook is a choice you can make at any time; second, the way to change one way of thinking is to substitute another way of thinking. Here's how you can apply these understandings.

- Consult what you've written so far in your notebook. Life is good, isn't it? If your page is still blank, now's the time to include a few entries; the more you make, the more fortunate you'll realize you are.

- Become curious about how many good and uplifting things are taking place around you. Maybe they're things you wouldn't normally have given a second glance, but now you notice.
- Entertain yourself with a game of positive substitutions. Be aware of negative sentiments or observations, and if they arise, immediately substitute a positive one that achieves the same end. Write it down. If you hear yourself saying, "I have so much work to do," write down what you've achieved to date instead.
- Focus on what is happening at this instant; enjoy every moment as it happens. (See "The moment is now" on page 243.)
- If you have a tendency to regret and to replay old events in your mind, keep focusing on the present. Alternatively, turn your thoughts forward. Create a mental picture of yourself in your most optimistic state, so you can be attracted by something inspiring.

Even though these steps appear simple, each has the power to change the way you look at life. Try them and you'll soon train yourself to recognize the positive side first. After a while it becomes habitual. You'll still see the things that go wrong, of course, but your focus will be biased toward how to make them right.

> The Calm Way: Your life will be as balanced as
> you make up your mind for it to be.

Calm for a balanced mind and spirit

This is one of the most important parts of this book. So important is it that I've written a number of books on this one topic: how to develop a sense of inner calm that can help you power through a busy, demanding life with ease and contentment.

Being able to enjoy such a state is beneficial not only to your physical health but to your mind and spirit as well. There are a number of ways to achieve it. Exercising and looking after your diet helps, as does having a positive and optimistic approach. But the way that follows is immensely more effective. Its power stems from a mix of indulgence and physiology.

The indulgent way

It's time to turn your attention to yourself—not to analyze what you're feeling or how you're coping with all this information, but to explore new ways of helping yourself feel balanced and fulfilled.

As the pace and pressure of everyday life carry us along, we tend to suppress our need for privacy and stillness. We get so caught up in the fervor of doing, as opposed to being, that we start to think of solitude as an absence of something rather than the presence of peace. But every human being needs space to let their guard down, forget about the ordeals of the day, and simply enjoy the pleasure of their own company. Even lonely people need to allow themselves this space.

With one simple diary entry, "Time to rebalance," you can create this space for yourself. Establish your own little oasis of peace that you can escape to and rediscover your inner strengths and vitality. Here you can unwind and recharge. You can be yourself. You can allow your mind and spirit the freedom they need to thrive.

"Time to rebalance" is explained in the Your Tools section on page 254. It takes only 20–30 minutes of your time. It requires no training and no special skills. And it has no inherent purpose other than to let you be yourself. Be relaxed. Be calm. Be restored.

"Time to rebalance" is more than just a way to relax. By relaxing and restoring order to your thoughts and physiology, you'll be able to approach the other activities of your day with increased energy, application, and enjoyment. So if you're the type who feels guilty about "doing nothing," tell yourself that this brief interlude will help you become more productive for the rest of the day. It will give you more energy and enthusiasm, and help bring balance to your life.

The parasympathetic way

Now we come to an ancient but extremely modern method of using calm to achieve a balanced mind and spirit. It's called "Deep Calm."

Deep Calm relates to your autonomic nervous system, another of your body's complex systems, which consists of two parts: the sympathetic and parasympathetic.

The sympathetic part helps you meet the demands of a busy, active life. To prepare you for emergency action, it speeds up your heart rate and blood flow, pumping a variety of "stress hormones" into your system. Usually this is accompanied by feelings of tension or fear. In an average stressful day, your sympathetic nervous system is working at full throttle.

Your *para*sympathetic system is the balancer of your nervous system. Its purpose is to compensate for all that stress and tension you produced. After you've been fired up, it helps you to cool down, conserve energy, and gradually return to normal. Ideally, it will cut in as soon as the action has passed. Unfortunately, a high-intensity workday doesn't allow you this luxury, so your parasympathetic system can remain inactive for long periods—hence the buildup of stress symptoms.

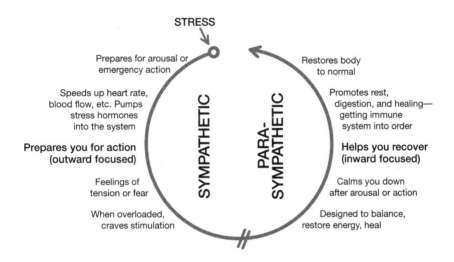

Deep Calm is a do-it-yourself intervention that replicates the actions of your parasympathetic nervous system. Deep Calm helps you relax and unwind. It reverses many of the negative effects of stress, and it enhances the efficiency of your immune system. If you approach it with an open mind, Deep Calm has the power to compensate for a high-pressure lifestyle or occupation and to help you cope with everyday problems and get more enjoyment and satisfaction out of life. And above all, it helps you to integrate all the different facets of your life—including all the skills and changes you are discovering in this book—into a balanced whole.

You can read about Deep Calm in the "Your tools" section on page 256. The benefits of Deep Calm are subtle and cumulative, much like an exercise program. It is at its most powerful when you

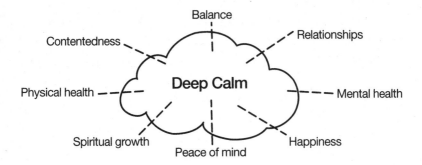

enjoy it for what it is, rather than for what it will do for you. And it really begins to pay off when you do it regularly for a reasonable length of time.

Service for a balanced spirit

You may be reading this book because of the work you do. What I'm going to suggest now involves a different kind of work. It's work that makes a difference. It helps people. It helps take your mind off problems you may be facing. It helps you to see your life in a broader context. And it helps you to maintain the balance between what you are, what you do, and the world you live in.

Whether this is visible to you or not, your world does enjoy a natural balance. From the smallest particle to the workings of the cosmos, balance is what everything is working toward. Isaac Newton first told us that for every action, there is an equal and opposite reaction. Modern science tells us of the perfect balance that exists between matter and anti-matter, between particles and anti-particles. Mathematics insists that both sides of an equation must be equal. Commercial enterprises insist that the sum of credits must equal the sum of debits on a balance sheet.

This is reciprocity. Reciprocity applies not only to science and nature but to most philosophical, ethical, and spiritual traditions. Despite great contrasts in beliefs and practices, the one principle most traditions have in common is the ethic of reciprocity. "Do unto others . . ." So, reciprocity is about more than just being compassionate and fair; it's ultimately about balance.

You may be wondering how this is going to help you make your life more balanced, especially when you consider that one of the primary sources of imbalance in life is the daily grind. You work in a competitive world. To get ahead, you have to be focused on your own needs and ambitions; you have to be assertive; you have to be first; you have to strain to get your way. Just trying to stay afloat can lead you to feel insular and self-absorbed.

But it doesn't have to be so one-sided. You can easily redress this imbalance and make a difference at the same time, by directing some of your efforts toward the benefit of others. In the spiritual world, this is known as service.

I'm not advocating that you do this for altruistic reasons. Do it because it will make you feel better and make your life more balanced. By putting effort into helping somebody else, you automatically overcome the sense of isolation that may accompany heavy workloads and responsibilities. On top of this is a sense of empowerment that comes from knowing you really can make a difference—maybe not to the whole world but certainly to an important part of it.

There's no need to go searching for world-changing causes to apply your talents to; you'll find real needs in your own neighborhood. Similarly, you don't have to turn this into a showpiece for a high achiever; trying to do too much only adds to the pressure you already labor under. Take it easy, act with compassion and sincerity, and be generous with help when help is needed.

This is how reciprocity will work for you.

The Calm Way: Help someone else, without expectation of reward, and you'll find it produces its own sense of joy and accomplishment.

Your body, mind, and spirit in balance

Establishing balance in your body, mind, and spirit is a dynamic process; sometimes you find it happening easily and fluidly; other times a little more patience may be required. On a day-to-day level you probably won't be aware of the changes taking place. In many ways it's like physical fitness: it's more noticeable when it's no longer there, such as when you fall ill or when you struggle to climb a flight of stairs. But someday in the not-too-distant future, you will compare the new you with the old one and will be thrilled with the transformation. Soon the process will become second nature to you. Soon you will rediscover that your natural state is one of balance. Be patient, and it happens. The change is already happening.

Now, as your body, mind, and spirit begin to sense this change—even if only in the most subtle way—it's time to move on to new discoveries and strategies that will help bring perfect balance to your life.

6.

PHASE 2:
Complete today's picture

Previously, you approximated your current state of life balance with a simple chart (page 63). Now it's time to take this a step further and to complete the picture. This will reveal which aspects of your life may be receiving too much or too little emphasis—essential knowledge if you're going to use this to make adjustments in the days ahead.

To do this, you need to identify:

- your main NEEDS in life
- the many different ROLES you play or feel you would like to play
- your main RESPONSIBILITIES.

You might wonder why more self-examination is necessary. "I'm working round the clock, my family is complaining, I have too many things to do in the time I have available, and there's only one of me to go around. I have a painfully clear idea of where my life balance stands right now."

But this view may not be as clear as you think.

For most of us, life is too frenetic to be able to pause and assess what's really going on while it's actually happening. We're too busy dealing with the events at hand. In addition, your world consists of not just a few different interests and responsibilities, but hundreds. These vary in importance according to what's happening today and the stage of life you're at. Even if you could grasp the full spread of them, your view might not be particularly reliable or objective because you are emotionally involved.

That's not all. To be able to function in a complex world, we have vast numbers of programmed responses that dictate how we act and think. If a car horn sounds on your left, you automatically swerve right—without thinking or evaluating. If someone mentions vinegar on strawberries, you automatically respond, "I don't like that"—without tasting. (You should try it sometime.) And if somebody questions your long work hours, you automatically say you have no option—it's a requirement of your job. These responses may once have had a purpose, but this can change over time.

Even if you could see through all these rote responses and put together what you believe is a complete list of your pressures and influences today, it won't look so complete when you review it tomorrow. Almost invariably you'll find there are some you've overlooked; probably many of them.

So let's start right at the beginning, with your needs.

The power of the list

Throughout this book you'll find many references to "make a list."
This has less to do with tidiness than it does with unloading concern.

It's a great way of putting things into perspective.
And of making problems appear less threatening. It's also
the way to order, and take the angst out of, worries.

And, best of all, all it takes is paper and pencil.
Such simple tools for such powerful results.

Your needs

Every reasonably well-balanced adult has a basic set of physical,
emotional, mental, and spiritual needs.

Broadly speaking, those that relate to self-interest (physical and
emotional) come first. When these are satisfied, you begin to focus
on the needs that relate to your role in the wider world.

Even within these broad frameworks, your individual needs have
a fairly specific ranking. Physical needs come first. When these are
satisfied, they immediately fade in importance and you move on to

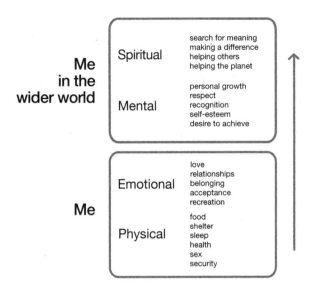

your emotional needs. When these are satisfied, you find yourself thinking about your mental needs. And only after these are satisfied do you move on to your spiritual needs.

If you haven't eaten for a few days and have been sleeping on a park bench, your physical need for food or shelter will be all you can think of. If you've eaten and slept well, these physical needs won't even enter your mind—you're too preoccupied with a cruel e-mail that came from your girlfriend this morning. Now your emotional needs are foremost in your mind.

If you've been eating and sleeping well, and have a satisfying relationship with your girlfriend, you might start thinking about that promotion you're going for at work—after all, much of your self-esteem is tied up in this (a mental need).

Taking this further: if you've been eating and sleeping well, have a satisfying relationship with your girlfriend, won the work promotion, and achieved most of the goals you set for yourself, you might suddenly feel . . . empty.

Now you're starting to feel the need to make a greater contribution to humankind, to make a difference with what you do; your spiritual needs are starting to dominate.

You won't be particularly aware of any of these basic needs if they're being satisfied. You will believe the next set of needs is more important. These are the ones that now occupy your attention, color your moods, and dictate your ability to enjoy life. These are the needs that should be managed if you are to find perfect balance.

> The Calm Way: If you want to change the reality you're focused on, simply focus on something more appealing.

The needs you're aware of

The needs you'll be most conscious of will be those applying pressure at the moment.

These tend to shift and change and vary in intensity, according to what's going on in your life. If you've been fired from your job and are struggling to pay the bills, your physical needs will suddenly become the most pressing. If you're recently divorced, your emotional needs might rise to the fore. If you're dissatisfied with your job, then it might be your mental needs. And if everything in life is nice and cozy, your spiritual needs will make their presence felt.

At other times it will be circumstances that make the difference. If you're suffering from a kidney ailment, your most pressing need might be health (a physical need). Or if you had an unhappy childhood, one of your major needs might be love (an emotional need). Or if you're desperate for a promotion in the job you've held for the past ten years, one of your primary needs might be respect or recognition (a mental need). And so on.

Just as each person is an individual, each person's needs are individual. Yours will vary according to your circumstances, occupation, colleagues, history (childhood, parents, upbringing, education, social status, etc.), as well as your wants and desires today. Soon we're going to make a list of these under the headings we've been using throughout this book: Physical, Spiritual, Work, Social.

To demonstrate how this list might finally appear, we can use the example produced by Mr. B, the university lecturer from page 32:

My most pressing PHYSICAL needs:
- reduce my stress levels
- feel fitter and more healthy
- cope better with my workload.

My most pressing SOCIAL needs:
- spend much more time with my family
- patch up my relationship with Debbie
- have my family understand the difficult time I'm going through
- be a comfort to my mother after her hip operation
- maintain contact with my golf buddies.

My most pressing WORK needs:
- prove my worth
- win the respect and support of my colleagues
- be appreciated for my efforts and experience.

My most pressing SPIRITUAL needs:
- I can't think of any at the moment.

Mr. B had two attempts at creating this list. His first focused less on his needs than his goals and ambitions. There is a big difference. Your needs are things that must be satisfied in order for you to survive, grow, and function reasonably well in the world. Your goals and ambitions are a wish list.

When putting together your list of needs, be aware of the difference between needs ("I need to . . .") and ambitions ("I want to . . ." or "I intend to . . .").

To make this step more enjoyable, why don't you pause for a while? Take a quiet half hour somewhere and just relax. Turn your thoughts to yourself and simply jot down what comes to mind when you say, "My most pressing physical needs are . . . " or "My most pressing social needs are . . ." And so on.

So you can feel relaxed while you do this, try not to force yourself to come up with answers. If nothing comes to mind in any specific area, don't worry. Just write down what comes to mind, and what's on your mind.

Once you have made your list, transpose it onto the following chart.

This list is only the beginning of the story. It's a snapshot of your needs today. At different times and different phases of your life, you may find that some needs will become less or more important than others. But, for now, this list is a great place to start.

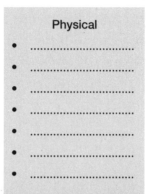

Physical

- ....
- ....
- ....
- ....
- ....
- ....
- ....

Work

- ....
- ....
- ....
- ....
- ....
- ....

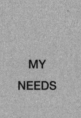

**MY
NEEDS**

Social

- ....
- ....
- ....
- ....
- ....
- ....

Spiritual

- ....
- ....
- ....
- ....
- ....
- ....
- ....

Your roles

Chances are that you will be a different person this afternoon than you were this morning. Tomorrow you will be different again. The difference may be subtle or pronounced, depending on the role you're playing.

Typically, the roles you play throughout the day could include:

- the family member—the parent, the grandparent, the partner, the lover, the son or daughter, the breadwinner, the homemaker
- the friend—the shoulder to cry on, the confidante, the person in need, the fun-lover
- the employee—the manager, the work colleague, the assistant, the super-executive, the underpaid or overworked worker
- the commuter, the restaurant patron, the concerned citizen, the taxpayer, the student, the flirt, the power walker, the dieter.

Each role has its own idiosyncrasies and pressures. When you're thinking of yourself in your parent role, you might resent spending one more minute at work than you absolutely have to. But if you're in your executive role, staying a few extra hours at work is simply the price of admission, and maybe even a welcome opportunity to get ahead.

When your roles occur more or less sequentially, they are fairly easy to manage. It's when they conflict or overlap that they cause problems. Imagine the following . . .

You're playing your domestic role. You're wearing your tattered bathrobe, watching a soap with your partner, eating pizza, and discussing bathroom renovations. There's a knock at the door. You open it, and there stands your most important client from work. What role are you playing now?

Or . . .

You're in your executive role, accompanying your CEO and an important client to dinner. Then just as the lobster arrives, so does the counselor who's been helping you work through a marriage problem. What role are you playing now?

All these different roles. Each one playing to a different audience. Each one bringing its own baggage and pressures. Each one introducing different demands and responsibilities. And unless you have a very clear idea of what you and your life are about, each one will be pulling you in a slightly different direction.

Balancing the roles

You shouldn't have much trouble listing the major roles you play in life. To get them into a more manageable perspective, we will segment them as before: the Physical roles, the Social roles, the Work roles, the Spiritual roles.

Beneath each of those primary roles is a range of sub-roles. These are the ones that occupy your everyday life (or you'd like them to at some time).

Before you start putting together your list, it might help to check out the various headings they're often arranged under.

PHYSICAL	SOCIAL	WORK	SPIRITUAL
Diet	Home and family	Achieving	Values
Health and exercise	Nonfamily relationships	Recognition and self-esteem	Search for meaning
Security	Part of a community	Producing	Making the world a better place
Rest		Other duties	Helping others
Recreation			Higher consciousness

A list of possible sub-roles follows. Almost certainly, your roles will differ from these, but use them to stimulate your thoughts when it comes to putting together your list.

PHYSICAL

- diet
  - the sensible eater
  - the diner
- health and exercise
  - the deskbound clerk
  - the daily walker
- security
  - the cleaner
  - the home renovator
- rest
  - the meditator
- recreation
  - the golfer
  - the adventurer

SOCIAL

- home and family
  - the parent
  - the partner/spouse
  - the child
  - the breadwinner
- nonfamily relationships
  - the best friend
  - the casual acquaintance
  - the workmate
- part of a community
  - the football coach
  - the fundraiser
  - the commuter

WORK

- achieving
  - the manager
  - the good assistant
  - the "I'll-do-it-at-home" exec.
- recognition and self-esteem
  - the reliable employee
  - the award winner
  - the MBA
  - the industry leader
- producing
  - the bookkeeper
  - the team leader
- other duties
  - the homemaker
  - the breadwinner
  - the home manager

SPIRITUAL

- values
  - the political activist
  - the philosopher
- search for meaning
  - the student
  - the spiritual seeker
  - the journal writer
- making the world a better place
  - the conservationist
  - the artist
- helping others
  - the charity worker
  - the volunteer
- higher consciousness
  - the music lover
  - the meditator

The words you choose to describe your roles, and even the categories they appear in, only have to be meaningful to you. For example, if you go to the office each day yet still do all the housework, you might see the role of "home manager" as being more appropriate to the Work category rather than the Social category. Similarly, you could also include "the breadwinner" role in either category. Just as each person and each person's life is different, so too are the roles they play and the interpretations of those roles.

If you take a look at the list of sub-roles prepared by Mr. C, the property group executive from page 35, you'll see he has included a number that might be considered more negative than positive.

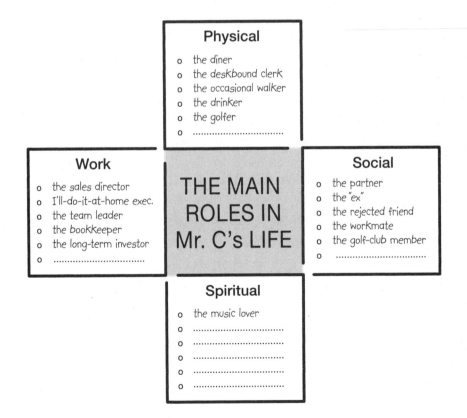

Physical

- o   the diner
- o   the deskbound clerk
- o   the occasional walker
- o   the drinker
- o   the golfer
- o   ....

Work

- o   the sales director
- o   I'll-do-it-at-home exec.
- o   the team leader
- o   the bookkeeper
- o   the long-term investor
- o   ....

THE MAIN ROLES IN Mr. C's LIFE

Social

- o   the partner
- o   the "ex"
- o   the rejected friend
- o   the workmate
- o   the golf-club member
- o   ....

Spiritual

- o   the music lover
- o   ....
- o   ....
- o   ....
- o   ....
- o   ....

Providing that this is an accurate assessment of his life today, there is no problem with this.

Now it's time for you to make a list of the major roles you play on a daily basis—the ones that occupy most of your time and attention.

Take a quiet half hour to do this. When you're nice and relaxed, turn your thoughts to yourself and the different roles you play. Write down whatever comes to mind when you say, "The main roles I play as a physical person are . . ." Or, "The main roles I play as working person are . . ." And so on.

If nothing springs to mind in any specific area, don't lose sleep over it. Just write down what comes to mind in another area, and move on.

Sometimes the roles you nominate will be too general to encompass all of what takes up your time. Consider, for example, the role of "the parent." What happens if you play a different role toward one child than another? Or if one of your children requires special attention, yet the others are just about ready to leave home and start careers? Or if you play a parental-type role to your nephew? In such a case you might subdivide your parent roles into "the parent," "the father of Lucy," and "the father-figure to Ben."

As well as the roles that presently take up your time and concentration, make sure you include those you haven't had time for lately, or those you aspire to or that you might not have adopted yet (such as "the nonsmoker").

When you've made your list, pare it down to the bare essentials and fill in the chart on the next page.

The Calm Way: When all roles you play come from the same script, you can perform them with poise and certainty.

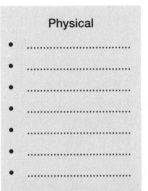

Physical
- ....
- ....
- ....
- ....
- ....
- ....
- ....

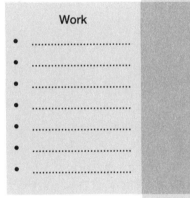

Work
- ....
- ....
- ....
- ....
- ....
- ....

**MY
ROLES**

Social
- ....
- ....
- ....
- ....
- ....
- ....
- ....

Spiritual
- ....
- ....
- ....
- ....
- ....
- ....
- ....

Your responsibilities

In an earlier chapter, we saw that much of the pressure you feel in life stems from conflicts between the things you want to do and the things you believe you have to do. Whether these obligations are specific or vague, they can weigh heavily on you, especially when you believe they're influenced by the needs and expectations of others.

You can make these responsibilities less abstract and more manageable by—you guessed it—making a list. So, bearing in mind that they will grow or shrink according to the circumstances of your life today, list your main responsibilities at the moment. This might include items such as your:

- work responsibilities (Work)
- professional obligations (Work)
- family responsibilities and duties (Social)
- partner responsibilities (Social)
- community responsibilities (Social or Spiritual)
- moral or ethical obligations (Spiritual)
- responsibilities for your personal development (Spiritual)
- responsibilities for your own health and well-being (Physical)
- financial debts (Physical).

Include them on the following chart.

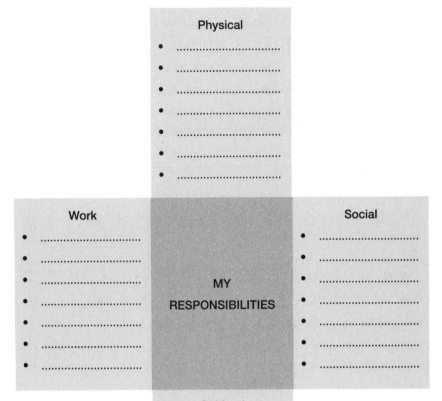

Looks a bit daunting, doesn't it? But you may be able to trim this list by examining your relationship with each of these responsibilities.

As we've been saying all along, your state of life balance is colored by the roles you play, shaped by the actions you take, and motivated by the needs you have. And it is greatly influenced by the responsibilities you believe you have.

Sometimes it is difficult to see that many of these responsibilities exist to satisfy *your* needs and drives. For example, the responsibility of providing for your family is one of your basic human needs, one that arises when your physical needs have been satisfied. Similarly, the community responsibilities you take on are one of your basic needs; you see the need for them only after your physical and emotional needs have been taken care of. Sure, your motivation may be altruistic and your actions may have enormous value, but you take on such responsibilities to satisfy needs of your own.

Recognizing this can remove a lot of the pressure that accompanies having many responsibilities. You'll feel much freer when you can say, "I'm doing this because I *choose* to," as opposed to, "I'm doing this because I *have* to."

The three lists

There you have it: your needs, your roles, your responsibilities. Three lists containing all the main pressures and influences in your life today. If you can think of any more, add them now.

You may be surprised by the volume of items you've included. So, before we move on to the next stage, take a couple of minutes to edit your lists. Delete everything you consider unimportant, irrelevant, or time-wasting.

> The Calm Way: The foundations of perfect balance are your own
> needs and actions. Once you accept responsibility for these,
> the rest fall into line.

Now, add some fun!

What you have in front of you is a summary of your life balance right now. Do you think it looks a little on the dry side? Do you think it needs more color and fun?

Of course it does! So this next small step is to inject a bit of that fun.

Refer back to your notebook from page 57 where you listed the fun and entertaining activities you indulge in. If you haven't made a list of them yet, here's your opportunity.

These are the things that add a bit of fun and enjoyment to my life:

- ....
- ....
- ....
- ....
- ....

We'll be referring back to this list later.

> The Calm Way: You don't have to look far to find joy and contentment.
> In fact, the instant you stop looking, you have them.

7.

PHASE 3:
Find your center of balance

It's so calm here, at the center.

Have you ever noticed what athletes do in the moments before they run onto the field? One slowly paces the changing room; another sits still, staring into thin air; another lies on a table, oblivious to all while a trainer massages her. Even though they all appear to be engaged in different activities, they are all really doing the same thing. They are using different techniques to center themselves.

It's not only athletes who do this. Musicians and actors center their emotions and energies before a demanding performance. Surgeons and therapists steal a few quiet moments to focus before attempting complex treatments. Soldiers strive to find their center before going into battle. Businesspeople try to center themselves before important negotiations. Just about everybody who is successful at what they do knows the importance of starting at that calm center.

It's just as vital when getting your life into balance.

There's something powerful and mystical about the center. The most stable part of a solid sphere is the center. The most stable position in any static object is the center of gravity. The most powerful place from which to direct action in martial arts is from the center. And, not surprisingly, the most serene and satisfying place to visit during meditation is the center.

Deep down, you are intuitively aware of what an extraordinary state exists there. If you pause—now—and think for a moment, where your center is, where you *feel* that it might be, you'll find your body has started to relax.

Did you notice that?

That's all you have to do—just turn your thoughts to where your center is—and your body begins to relax. You can actually feel your pulse beginning to slow. Your breathing is getting quieter.

Now you know why we call this your calm center.

There is no other kind of center but calm. It's the point where your whole being becomes tranquil and still, when your attention moves from the past or future to right now, when you are in touch with all your inner resources, when you are perfectly balanced to move this way or that as circumstances demand. It's also the place where all of your life's efforts and concerns come together—integrate, if you wish—and suddenly make sense.

We call this your center of balance.

In the next section we're going to determine where your center of balance is. Following this, in Phase 4 we will create a "balance reference point," a convenient reminder of what's important in your life—one that you can refer back to at any time, such as when you're busy or under pressure or just lose the plot.

Finding your center of balance

Here is the one point in your world where you feel centered and in control. Perhaps you don't know exactly where or what it is right now, but you sense that such a place exists.

Your center of balance may be physical, emotional, philosophical, or spiritual. More than likely, it will be a combination of these. But once you know where it is or what it is, it becomes the fulcrum for your life's efforts and concerns.

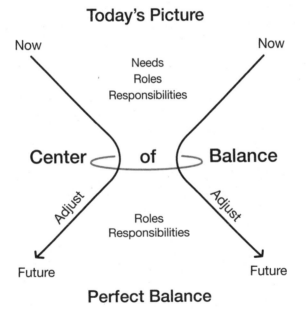

Your center of balance helps you bring into focus all the many needs, roles, and responsibilities in your life. It helps you determine what roles can be downplayed or shed and what adjustments might be made to the remainder so that you can work toward achieving perfect balance.

You start with your list of needs, roles, and responsibilities from the previous chapter. You compare them with your center of balance. Then you fine-tune or adjust in an orderly way.

Do you already have a center of balance?

Somewhere, sometime, most people have an experience that colors every other aspect of their life for a while.

You're in a hot new relationship. Or your first child is born. Or you take on an exciting new job. Or you develop a passion for a new pastime or activity that occupies your every thinking moment. Or you lose a few pounds, and for the first time in your life you can see muscle tone in your abdomen and arms. Or you get involved in a cause that seems the most important thing on earth. Or you get a great promotion and can see only riches and power ahead.

Peak events such as these happen only a few times in your life, and the gaps between them grow larger as you mature.

Peak events become personal benchmarks. They bring a rosy new perspective to your world. When they occur, all other activities and responsibilities seem to fall smoothly and conveniently into place around them.

Can you remember such a feeling? Even though your new promotion meant you were working harder than ever before, you suddenly seemed to have more energy and enthusiasm for other activities. Or, even though your new baby had no relationship whatsoever with work, your job suddenly seemed more meaningful and important. Even though your work award had little to do with your domestic life, suddenly you found more joy and satisfaction in your relationship with your partner.

And why not! At times like this you feel that your life is in order.

You're in the zone. Everything is just right. You have energy to spare. Nothing is beyond your capabilities. You feel stable and centered. And deep down, you feel that it will continue like this forever.

You can imagine how powerful you'd be if you could maintain that state as an anchor, or a balance point, for all your life activities. It could become a physical, emotional, and spiritual reminder of why you go to work each day, why you come home at night, and why you strive to stay healthy. If the event that caused this feeling was new and exciting, maybe you could.

But only for a while.

As inspiring and empowering as such events may be, they ultimately fall short of being the long-term stabilizing influence you imagined. Somehow your hot new romance morphs into a comfortable, routine relationship. Or your innocent little baby grows into an argumentative teenager. Or the new job becomes predictable and repetitive. Then, what you thought was your center of balance starts to lose its power to motivate.

There's a rule I learned very early in business: never base your plans on phenomena or peak events. In the main, they can't be reproduced or sustained. This is why the peak events in your life do not make a suitable center of balance on a long-term basis.

Where to find your center of balance

Your center of balance is an imaginary place or a state where all of your life's responsibilities and interests merge and make sense.

Even if you knew where to start looking for it, you might not easily recognize it. Yet it could appear in all kinds of different forms: physical (a picture of your new baby or your dream home), emotional (the thought of your lover or a quest to help starving children in a Third World country), philosophical (fighting corruption or spreading calm), or spiritual (finding enlightenment or serving your god). Your center of balance could even be an attitude or a state of mind.

Ideally, it will be a combination of all of these and will take into account every facet of your life, starting with the needs, roles, and responsibilities you identified in the previous chapter.

Following is a simple process that will help you define your center of balance. Its starting point is to determine your life's priorities—as they are now and will be in the future—and to identify any purpose you feel you have.

Sorting your priorities

Most people have a rough idea of what their priorities are. These will be a summary of their most obvious needs, roles, and responsibilities.

What are your priorities? Do they include your family? Your job? Your relationships? The role you play in the community? If you have difficulty identifying your priorities through a simple deductive process, you may need to apply a little imagination.

The Calm Way to do this is through a variation on the "Go forward, step back" technique on page 252. Imagine yourself on your eightieth birthday: you are reflecting on the life you've led, the relationships you've had, and the things you've experienced. Take time to relax; you have all this spare time on your hands. What do you look like at this age? How do you sound? What are your surroundings? Come on, let your imagination drift. No time pressures, no future pressures. All you have to do is sit there—relaxing, imagining . . .

Now, look back over your life. What made you happy? What made you feel satisfied and fulfilled? Was it your career? The wealth you amassed? Was it that you spent your best moments with your children or fostering your relationships? Was it that you achieved the best you were capable of in most undertakings? Was it that you made a difference to the world at large, to your community, or to your family and friends? What's most important to you now on your eightieth birthday?

Without any kind of analysis, as quickly and as fluidly as you can, write down the priorities that come to mind. This will help you bypass the intellectual clutter and develop a better idea of what's important in your life—deep down as well as on the surface. List your priorities in the order that *feels* right.

The priorities in my life are, in order:

- ....
- ....
- ....
- ....
- ....

Adding value

Your list of priorities can be refined even further by keeping only those that harmonize with your values.

What are your core values? This is a question that most people go through life without ever asking. Yet values are what give your life direction and meaning and make you the person you are. Even when you're not aware of them, you're always applying them—to evaluate your thoughts, to distinguish right from wrong, to know one course of action is preferable to another. They begin to form at an early age and evolve as you get older.

If you haven't spent time thinking about your core values, it's not always easy to work out what they are. Sometimes it helps to think about those of someone you admire—a relative, a colleague or acquaintance, a teacher, a historic figure. You don't really have to know the person, just know enough about them to be able to isolate what their values are.

What are their qualities you admire most? Is it their integrity? Is it their truthfulness, compassion, or love of life? If you can't find a word that summarizes these values, but you have a *feeling* for what they mean to you, try to describe it. Jot down your thoughts here.

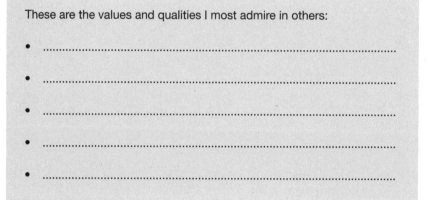

These are the values and qualities I most admire in others:

- ....
- ....
- ....
- ....
- ....

This will put you more in the frame of mind to consider the qualities and values that shape *your* life.

These are the values and qualities that feature in my life:

- ....
- ....
- ....
- ....
- ....

Now take those two lists and narrow down all the items to the two or three you *feel* are most important to you.

These are the values and qualities most important to me:

- ....
- ....
- ....

The last step is to go back to your list of life priorities (page 143) and see how they stack up against your core values.

You may find that some are not overly compatible. For example, if one of your priorities was "accumulating wealth," and one of your life's values was "thrift and modesty," you'd have a conflict. Fortunately, this is easily resolved by revising one of them: probably your priority.

What's your purpose?

Do you know of anyone who has an ideally balanced life—where their work, personal life, and spiritual fulfillment blend comfortably together, and there's plenty of time left over for recreation and other pursuits?

This will not be a person who lurches from one day to the next without direction or intention; if there's one quality almost every well-balanced life possesses, it's a sense of purpose. Certainly, the successful, fulfilled people that I've encountered have had it.

Where does a clear and meaningful sense of purpose come from?

For a start, it's much broader than what you do for a living or what you plan to do in the future. It relates to the central motivation in your life. When you understand it, it becomes almost like a mini-manual for living. It provides direction for your actions and decisions. It keeps you on track. It motivates. It can even become your center of balance. Yet if you ask most people what their purpose is, you'll get a blank look.

As a step toward introducing more balance into your life, it will pay to explore what *your* purpose is. This doesn't have to involve a lot of effort or soul-searching, just a few relaxed minutes on your favorite topic: you.

Broadly speaking, a description of your life purpose will encompass your priorities and values—if not in words, then certainly in sentiment.

It doesn't have to be a grand or unique statement. Most descriptions of life purpose are relatively mundane to the rest of the world, but compelling and motivating for the originator.

Whether your purpose is to teach or to heal, or to use your wealth to make a better world for everyone, or to be caring and loving toward everyone you come in contact with, the only measure that counts is whether it is meaningful and motivating for you.

Usually your purpose will reflect the qualities, passions, and talents that make you who you are, as well as the things you feel most strongly about.

Can you think of a phrase or sentiment that sums up the motivation for your life? Go for a slow, relaxing walk and take half an hour to think about it.

The Calm Way: The more you care about the result,
the more certain you are of attaining it.

Were there any events, experiences, or achievements that you found to be particularly moving or fulfilling? Were there occasions when you felt powerful and effective? Have you ever thought what mark you'd like to leave in your immediate world?

If you're receptive to an answer, one will come. When it does, you'll recognize it by the fact that just the mere thought of it motivates you, makes you feel fulfilled even before you put it into play, and maybe even scares you a little.

This is your purpose. If nothing comes to mind, don't worry. In time it will happen.

The Calm Way: Can you sense where your center might be at
this instant? The moment your thoughts take you there,
you feel centered.

Pulling it all together

You summarized all your different needs, roles, and responsibilities when you created your list of priorities. You refined this by comparing it with your values.

You may then have summarized all of these with a simple statement about your life's purpose.

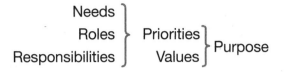

Now it's time to move on from the abstract into something more concrete. We're going to turn all these hazy or not-so-hazy concepts into something you can look at and touch.

Your Balance Vision

Note: The following step requires courage. Some people are reluctant to expose themselves in the way it requires, and they will find any excuse to avoid doing so. Do I dare create this picture of what I could be? What if I fail? What if I do it and nothing changes? What if I start down this path then realize what I had was better? So they protest that they don't have the time or don't think it's important, or something along those lines. You know, of course, that these excuses are just avoidance. I urge you to ignore them. Push on with confidence, and watch how your life begins to change.

Your Balance Vision is a physical reminder of all that's important and meaningful in your life. It may take an hour or so to work through and prepare, but this should be entertaining, and it will certainly be worth the time you invest.

Earlier we mentioned how peak events in life might serve as a center of balance for you, at least for a while. An example of this was the birth of a child.

Many new parents find that a desk photo of their child would serve as a physical reminder of what they are working and striving for. It might keep them energetic and enthusiastic throughout their

working day. It might direct their attention to that part of their life where they feel centered, useful, and in control.

And when times get tough and they lose sight of what is important in their world, all they have to do is glance at this little framed picture and everything falls into place again.

Your Balance Vision will work just like this, but on a more sustainable basis.

What does your vision look like?

Your Balance Vision is a more interesting and memorable summary of the topics we've been through in recent pages:

- Your life balance—as you want it to be
- Your priorities, values, and purpose.

Even though the word "vision" implies pictures or graphics, a Balance Vision can take many different forms. It could be a snippet of hair in a locket, a few seconds of audio on your computer, some well-chosen words, a perfume-soaked scarf, an icon, a sculpture, a drawing or painting . . . there's no limit to the possibilities. All that's important is that this vision is meaningful and motivating for you. You are the only judge.

Generally, you will choose either a visual or a verbal way of conveying this. It's a matter of personal choice. Do you thrive on the power and evocativeness of imagery? Or do you require the literalness of words?

"The image of a Balance Vision" is the visual approach; it relies on photos, graphics, symbols, and possibly even material objects.

Visual ? ? ? Verbal

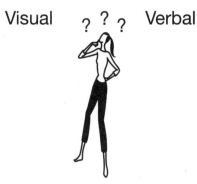

"The description of a Balance Vision" is the verbal approach; it relies on words.

Each vision fulfills the same function, and each is as useful as the other. As long as it is memorable, easily understood, and motivating for you, either would be appropriate. Choose whichever one you feel most comfortable with, and try to incorporate the following characteristics.

- VISUAL, so it appeals to the nonjudgmental side of your thinking (right brain) and is easier to recall. Even if you've chosen the verbal approach, you may be able to find words that evoke mental images.
- EMOTIONAL, so that it makes you *feel* something, rather than appealing to your intellect.
- MOTIVATIONAL, so it makes you want to move forward.

What you're about to embark on is a dynamic process. Your Balance Vision may turn out to be absolutely perfect first go, or it may require modifications in the future. This is all part of the fun of it and what makes it interesting for you. But the wonderful thing is, you can't lose: once you're on the path, the process itself provides direction.

> The Calm Way: To turn an idea into a reality, get your
> subconscious to take over the task. The easiest
> way to do this is through your imagination.

The image of a Balance Vision

If you ever suspected there was a bit of a van Gogh lurking inside you, now's the time to set him free. We're going to summarize your priorities, values, and purpose in a graphic form, with colors, symbols, and powerful images. If you include words, they will be short, bold, and fun (no small writing, no long sentences). Forget about artistic quality and have fun creating it.

- Start by placing a photograph of yourself in the center of a large sheet of blank paper. Choose the photograph for the feeling it creates: happy and content will serve you better than handsome or slim.
- Next, add a visual reminder of the main priority in your life, from the top of the list you created on page 143. If there's a relationship between this and your other priorities, you can include them as well. Be sparing here because we're trying to keep this simple.
- If you've worked out your sense of purpose, add it as well.
- Include anything that you think should receive special attention, or adds enjoyment, or will help you satisfy your priorities and live up to your purpose.
- Fine-tune all of these elements on the page to ensure that they sit comfortably with your core values.

The following graphic example was prepared by Mr. B, the university lecturer we mentioned on page 32. If you compare it with his needs list (page 122), you'll see a strong relationship between the two. Because his work already dominated, there was no need for him to make any further allowance for it. His ideal was to focus more on his family and home life, as well as other things that give his life meaning.

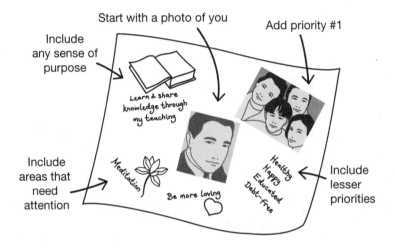

At the top right, Mr. B highlighted his priorities. These are all family-based: first comes their health and happiness; then, to satisfy his own needs as a good provider, comes his children's education and paying off the mortgage.

Top left is his sense of purpose: to "learn & share knowledge through my teaching."

Mr. B's three main core values are "compassion," "sharing," and "learning." Even though these are not literally represented here, they're reflected in the style and tone of the rest of his graphic: healthy—happy—family—be more loving—meditation—learn—share knowledge.

One area that he thought required special attention was his health, primarily the stress levels from his work. He decided that the way of dealing with this, as well as enriching the spiritual side of his life, was to learn to meditate. Hence the word "meditation" on the bottom left.

Finally, at the base of his graphic Mr. B added: "be more loving." This was included for personal reasons he did not wish to elaborate on.

The description of a Balance Vision

Not everyone feels at home with graphics; they prefer the comfort and precision of words for their Balance Vision. In the corporate world we're quite used to having visions communicated in words rather than pictures.

Your "Description of a Balance Vision" is a two- or three-paragraph statement that sums up all of what would be covered in the visual version. The phrases and expressions you use should be personal, positive, and in the present tense. If you wish to make them visually oriented, use words such as "see," "view," and "color." The literary quality is much less important than the sentiment.

- Start with the words "My life is in perfect balance because . . ."
- Add something about the main priority in your life and how you feel about it. If there is a relationship between this and your other priorities, make reference to them.
- If you've worked out your sense of purpose, include it as well. "My purpose is . . ."
- Include anything you think should receive special attention or will help you satisfy your priorities and live up to your purpose.
- Fine-tune all of these elements on the page to ensure that they sit

comfortably with your core values. Because we're dealing with a more literal interpretation here, you can include these as well. "My values are . . ."

Had Mr. B prepared his Balance Vision as a statement, it would have looked something like this:

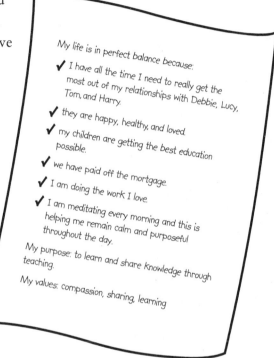

My life is in perfect balance because:

✔ I have all the time I need to really get the most out of my relationships with Debbie, Lucy, Tom, and Harry.

✔ they are happy, healthy, and loved.

✔ my children are getting the best education possible.

✔ we have paid off the mortgage.

✔ I am doing the work I love.

✔ I am meditating every morning and this is helping me remain calm and purposeful throughout the day.

My purpose: to learn and share knowledge through teaching.

My values: compassion, sharing, learning

One last note: what you write here may seem unimaginative and maybe even predictable. This is not uncommon; nor is it a concern. You've been shaping your thoughts and priorities as you made your way through this book, so it's only natural that there will be a degree of familiarity to your words. If you want to add more color, do it with colored pencils, photographs, fancy borders, or any other element that will make your vision more distinctive.

Making it portable

Having completed these steps—either visually or verbally—you now have your first attempt at a Balance Vision. Remembering that most people have at least a couple of attempts before they're satisfied, you're ready to put it to work.

The intention of your Balance Vision is to instantly remind you why you go to work and come home each day. If things go off the rails, or your motivation drains, or you feel you're doing too much of one thing and not enough of another, a single glimpse at this special reminder should help you to feel centered, useful, and in control.

Naturally, this is only going to happen when you're thoroughly familiar with its content—when you can shut your eyes and still see it; when you can visualize it in the traffic or at the supermarket or in the boardroom. To build this kind of familiarity you need to see it over and over. And the simplest way to do this is to create a mini-version: a playing-card-sized copy of the original. Any photocopying service can do this for you. Even if it is too small to see all the details, it still works as an instant reminder.

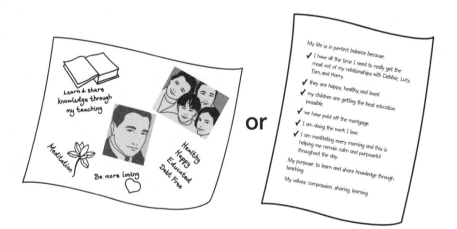

The final and important step is to refer to it often. Leave a copy in your desk drawer, by your bedside table, on your bathroom mirror, or in your handbag or briefcase. The more your Balance Vision is embedded in your consciousness, the more effectively it will work for you.

Is this vision a goal?

Having well-defined goals is a prerequisite to success in almost all avenues of life. You could say that your Balance Vision is a goal of sorts—a big-picture goal.

But rather than looking at it in this way, try to see it as an emotional state or feeling you can attain and sustain. Sometimes you may have to satisfy a few goals to be able to feel this way, but in the main, this happens in your head.

Try it.

Imagine, right now, that you can perform a miracle. With a click of your fingers you can totally change your view of life. Instead of feeling stretched and pressured, you suddenly feel you have all the time to do whatever you want to do. Instead of feeling torn between this responsibility and that, you suddenly feel you can accommodate every one of them, and love every moment of doing so. If you could perform that miracle, wouldn't you say your life was more balanced?

Perfect balance is as much a state of mind as any kind of accomplishment. That "miracle" you just imagined is not only achievable, it is precisely where you're headed now. The time will come when this state of mind will exist, regardless of the goals you set or the events and details of your everyday life.

Paradoxically, once this state of mind exists, all your smaller goals become easier to accomplish. They become the minutiae of day-to-day life, as you live out the big-picture ideal defined in your Balance Vision. We will address these goals in the next chapter.

(When you do get to the stage where you want to formulate goals, use the "Setting goals" method on page 259.)

8.

PHASE 4:
Adjust the balance

You now have a fair idea of the center of balance in your life—the place where everything seems to make sense and hold together. You summarized this in your Balance Vision. This now becomes the point around which you reconfigure your life pressures and influences, and reweight your roles and activities.

The good news is that this reconfiguring does not always involve major change to your lifestyle or work style; it may be more about minor adjustments to perceptions and priorities. This is why we refer to this process as *adjusting* the balance.

Until now we've been dealing at arm's length with the issues and subtleties that make you the unique person you are. Apart from the foundation steps of getting your body, mind, and spirit in balance, we've mostly been dealing in theory, plans, and strategies.

Now it's crunch time. Perfect balance is in sight. To make it a reality you now have to make some real decisions and commitments. This is where you start making actual adjustments in your occupations and preoccupations—*not always by reducing or shedding activities but occasionally by adding them!* In some instances, this may require discipline, maybe even a little sacrifice and courage from you.

However, as you now have perfect balance in mind, this will be easier than you think.

But what do you balance? Do you try to juggle all the hundreds of interests and responsibilities? Do you modify your personal needs and ambitions according to what seems feasible and appropriate? Preferably not, because if ever there were a hard way to try to balance your life, this would be it.

The Calm Way doesn't attempt to balance all the various activities and subtleties that occur within your various roles, it simply rebalances the roles and your attitudes toward them.

> The Calm Way: Instead of trying to balance the activities within each of the roles you play, rebalance the roles.

Balancing your primary roles

We've been talking a lot about roles throughout this book. There are two ways to look at these: from a big-picture perspective (your primary roles) and from a detailed perspective (your sub-roles).

For the moment we're going to focus on the big picture—your primary roles of Physical, Social, Spiritual, Work—and adjust the balance between them.

To visualize these adjustments, we'll use a sliding scale graphic similar to the one on the following page.

Each line represents a particular role: Physical, Social, Spiritual, Work. By changing the position of the "sliders" by whatever degree you feel necessary, you can rearrange the importance of each role—giving it more emphasis or less, according to what you believe is ideal.

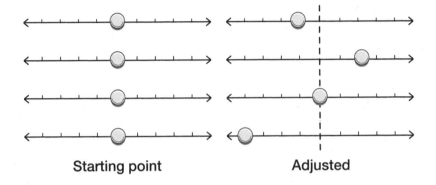

Your starting point will have all sliders in a neutral, midway position. This represents neither balance nor imbalance; it simply illustrates where your life balance stands *right now*.

Unless you already have a perfectly balanced life, the emphasis of each role will need to be adjusted before it achieves the ideal in your Balance Vision. Simply use a pen or a pencil to illustrate this move as in the example above.

Bear in mind that each line has a relationship to the others. When you add to one, you take from the others. If you move one ahead two notches, you need to move another *back* two notches to balance it. (Or move two of them back a notch.) While there's no need to be mathematically perfect, it does help to maintain the ratios as best you can.

Primary role	Ratio

The above example was prepared by Ms. A, the divisional director of a financial services institution we discussed on page 30. In making these sliding adjustments, Ms. A's Physical roles remained unchanged, her Social roles were given much more emphasis, her Spiritual roles received a little more, and her Work roles were reduced substantially. That's her idea of a perfectly balanced life.

Your idea of a perfectly balanced life will be different from Ms. A's, but you can see how easily this process works in principle.

Now it's time to make the adjustments to *your* primary roles.

Start with your reference point

Before you pick up your pencil, you need a reference point. Earlier, you created an abstract big-picture view of your life balance as you want it to be. You also created a more refined and humanized version of this, your Balance Vision. For now, either or both of these will serve as your reference point as you adjust the weightings of your primary roles.

First, pause for a few minutes to allow your mind to clear.

Refer to your Balance Vision or your "Life balance—as you want it to be" chart. Then, with a pencil and the following sliding scale chart, make whatever role adjustments are needed to produce the kind of balance you think would be perfect.

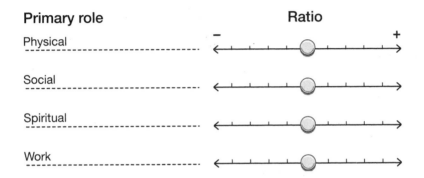

> The Calm Way: When you can see the opposites in your life as complementary forces rather than conflicting ones, you have a view of perfect balance.

Balancing your sub-roles

Now that you have a big-picture view of the adjustments you're going to make to your *primary* roles, you can adjust the balance of your *sub*-roles.

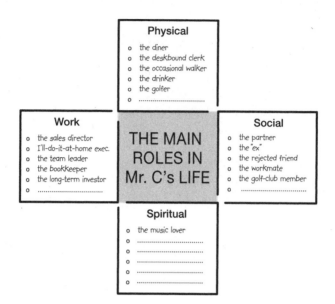

These are the ones you listed on page 131 under the primary headings of Physical, Social, Work, and Spiritual. These are the individual roles you play throughout your day, which occupy most of your time and attention. They may also include roles you aspire to or haven't had time to concentrate on lately.

You're going to use the sliding scale device to rebalance each of these within the context of your primary role.

My Physical roles

In a moment you're going to list the major physical roles in your life. To illustrate how this works, take a look at how Ms. I—the full-time homemaker and mother of a six-year-old and a toddler (on page 46)—described hers.

On the first line she wrote "the sensible eater" because it was a matter that had been weighing on her mind. Next she added "the regular exerciser" as a role because, although she seldom exercised, it was something she regularly thought about. On the third line she wrote "the soap addict," in recognition of the fact that she wasted a couple of hours each day watching television shows that she considered time-wasting and trivial. (You might not define this as a physical role, but each person sees their roles differently.) And on the fourth line she wrote "the food-lover" because she and her husband had devoted so much time and money to this pursuit in recent times.

Having listed these Physical roles, Ms. I then consulted her Balance Vision. This would guide her decisions on how she should re-assign her time and efforts among her Physical roles.

It was definitely time to get her diet in order, so Ms. I moved the first slider to the +3 position. It was also time to start exercising more, so she advanced that slider as well. The "soap addict" role was marked for reduction, as was "the food-lover" role because it was probably contributing to her weight problem. This is how her final chart looked:

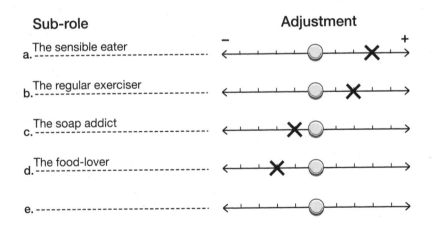

Now that you've seen how Ms. I did it, you can list the major Physical roles *you* play, or aspire to, in life.

Once you have done this, adjust the sliders one way or the other to illustrate the balance that you feel is appropriate.

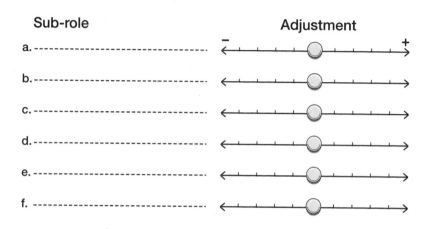

My Social roles

This encompasses your role as a family member as well as a member of a group. Write down the major roles from your list (page 131).

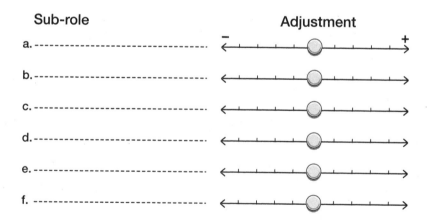

Adjust the sliders to illustrate the emphasis you feel is appropriate.

My Spiritual roles

Depending on the stage of life you're at, this could be a well-populated section or very thin.

Write down the major spiritual roles from your list (page 131).

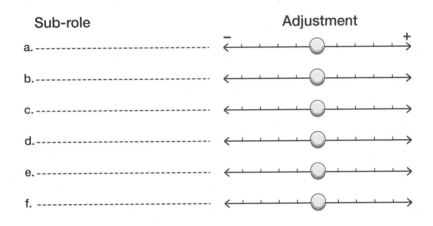

Adjust the sliders to illustrate the emphasis you feel is appropriate.

My Work roles

This should be the easiest to compile because there are so many roles, duties, and responsibilities you have to manage in your day-to-day work.

Write down the major ones from your list (page 131).

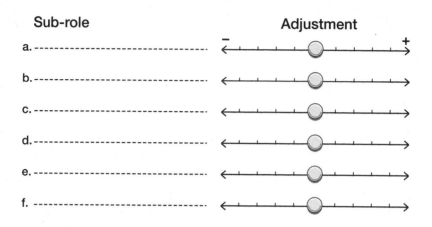

	Sub-role	Adjustment

Adjust the sliders to illustrate the emphasis you feel is appropriate.

The four modes of adjustment

Now that you know the *emphasis* you want to give each role, it's time to go about actually adjusting them in your life. There are three ways to do this.

- You make physical changes.
- You make attitudinal changes.
- Other people change.

The hard way to attempt such changes is to try to force yourself to make them. The Calm Way is a more relaxed approach that gives you a choice of four "adjustment modes," which we've categorized as heads, hearts, clocks, and negotiation.

Heads

Heads relate to the plans, decisions, and strategies you formulate using your brainpower. These are the more logical and rational steps you can take.

Hearts

The psychological, intuitive, or emotional approaches can be more powerful. These can be the difference between one person being delighted with what they have (a job, for instance), while another person in the same position thinks it's the pits.

Clocks

Most people insist on believing they have too little time available to do what they have to do or that they have too much to do in the time they have available. When that attitude persists, the only way around it is through scheduling—or rescheduling.

Negotiation

Finally, when your plans are in place and you feel in control of your work and schedules, yet you can't accommodate all of the demands or expectations of others, you'll have to negotiate your way through the issues that confront you.

The Calm Way uses some of these modes, or all of them, depending on your preference. We will explore each of these in the pages ahead.

Heads

There are three primary ways to adjust your life roles:
you make physical changes, you make attitudinal
changes, or other people make the changes.

With your Balance Vision and your sliding scale results, you can now start formulating plans and strategies for achieving perfect balance. As this point will involve some detail, you'll probably be more comfortable using your head rather than your emotions to find the solutions.

The following methods are called "Role strategies" and "Life editing." Besides helping you to get your various roles in order, they'll help you save time and clear some of the clutter from your world.

Role strategies

Earlier you produced four sliding scale charts of your sub-roles. These show the areas of your life you've chosen to adjust and the degree of adjustment you intend. Each adjustment now becomes an individual goal you've set.

For every goal you have in life, you need a strategy, regardless of whether this goal is general ("A lot less meeting time, a lot more selling time") or specific ("One hour less in sales meeting, one hour more in face-to-face sales").

Let's use the example of Mr. C's Work roles from page 129. You'll recall that Mr. C is an executive in the group that manages large shopping centers. The roles he listed were: the sales director, the I'll-do-it-at-home exec., the team leader, the bookkeeper, and the long-term investor. When he adjusted these Work roles to reflect a more balanced ideal, his chart looked like the one on the following page.

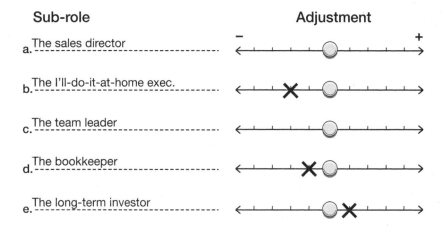

Sub-role	Adjustment

Each of these adjustments requires a strategy if it is to be fulfilled.

If Mr. C intends to reduce the emphasis of his I'll-do-it-at-home exec. role (b), he needs a strategy for how he's going to accomplish it. When is he going to complete his work? How will he have to change his workday to be able to accommodate this?

If he's going to increase his long-term investor role (e), he needs a strategy for this as well. What kind of investments? What objective? What resources will he need? How much extra time will it take?

And the same applies to the other roles he intends to change.

Trying to adjust your roles without a strategy will only add to the pressure you feel you're under, and it can lead to unpredictable results. Use a strategy that incorporates the following characteristics and you'll be more certain to succeed.

It must be POSITIVE. Psychologically, you will feel more motivated to do something that is phrased positively rather than negatively. You find it easier to follow a moderate diet than to lose weight. You find it easier to go home earlier than to work fewer hours. You find it easier to take up meditation than to stop feeling stressed.

Second, it must be SPECIFIC. You must be able to determine

how and when it will be achieved. It's difficult to effect a strategy like "I'll work less," because it's general and vague. But when you make it more specific—such as "I will finish work on time at least three days a week"—you'll find it much easier to pull off.

Strategies for your Physical roles

What strategies would you employ to make the adjustments shown on your Physical chart? How will you be able to find time or resources needed to implement them?

While your strategies will be determined by your own particular decisions and circumstances, here are a few examples of what other people chose for theirs.

- Set aside time for personal pampering, such as a regular massage.
- Move your diet in the direction of wholefoods and plant-based foods, keeping portions at a reasonable level and avoiding fatty, preserved, and refined foods.
- Learn to meditate or at least set aside a period of quiet time each day that you can designate for "Time to rebalance" (page 254).
- Have physical check-ups from time to time but focus on prevention rather than cure for your ongoing wellness.
- Keep physically active, and find an exercise that you'll enjoy and participate in regularly.
- Find ways to enjoy life that don't depend on excessive alcohol or drugs.
- Become a nonsmoker.
- Plan a schedule that allows plenty of rest and keeps stress under control.
- Work at seeing the positive side of life and maintaining an optimistic attitude.

Now that you have the general idea, go ahead and start making a list of your strategies. This may be a list you add to or modify as you work your way through this book.

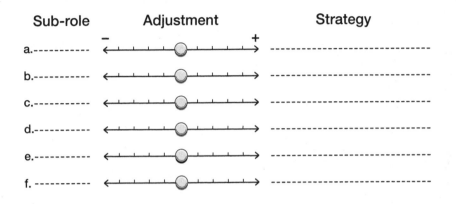

Strategies for your Social roles

What strategies would you employ to make the adjustments shown on your Social chart? How can you satisfy your own needs and expectations at the same time as you do so for others?

Here are a few examples of what other people chose for their strategies in this category.

- Plan a few weekends away with your spouse or partner.
- Have regular family meetings so you can make joint decisions and share responsibilities.
- Make a practice of having meals at whatever hour enables the family to be together.
- Share information with other family members so they understand the stresses you encounter at work.
- Establish support systems—such as babysitting, parent-sitting, carpools, and responsibility-swapping—that will help you make your workload more manageable.

- Share household tasks and childcare (sharing workloads and responsibilities with your partner is a great way to keep job pressures in perspective).
- Make regular "dates" with each of your children, parents, and friends, so you can have relaxed, ongoing involvement in their lives.
- Establish and maintain community links in the areas that appeal to you or that you feel strongly about.

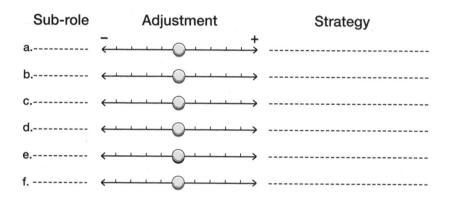

Strategies for your Spiritual roles

What strategies would you employ to make the adjustments shown on your Spiritual chart? How can you fulfill some of your more elevated ambitions, without neglecting other areas?

Here are a few examples of what other people chose for their strategies in this category.

- Meditate regularly to become a happier, more content person.
- Make an effort to identify your core values and strive to live by them.
- Use your faith or beliefs to keep the rest of your life in perspective.
- Do what you can to keep the earth healthy and vibrant; support conservationist issues where appropriate.

- Take on additional studies to enrich or improve yourself.
- Go to the theater.
- Keep a journal as a way of sorting through your thoughts and feelings.
- Find a way of sharing your knowledge, experience, or good fortune with others who can grow by it.
- Become a charity volunteer.
- Have lots of friends and be active in the way you care for them.
- Spread peace and love wherever possible.
- Write a book, paint a picture, tend a garden.

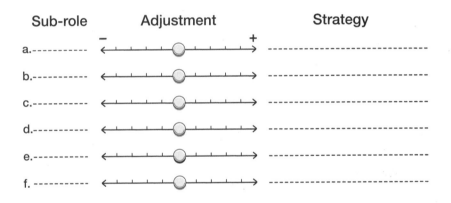

Strategies for your Work roles

What strategies would you employ to make the adjustments shown on your Work chart? How can you limit the impact these might have on other areas of your life?

Here are a few examples of what other people chose for their strategies.

- If you can see no relief in your current job, consider changing positions, shifts, hours, or even employers to find what you're looking for.

- Explore flexitime arrangements with your employer, varying your start or finish times to suit your needs.
- Consider telecommuting or part-telecommuting as a way of reducing travel time or helping with family commitments.
- Negotiate job-sharing or part-time working arrangements to free up time for other needs or responsibilities.
- Renegotiate workloads or timing requirements if these become too burdensome.
- Develop new skills and credentials that will enhance your progress or enjoyment of your work.
- Find ways to allow lots of little successes throughout your workday.
- Take a short break every 90 minutes or so to get your thoughts in order and to look at the positive side of what you're doing.
- Work one task, one day at a time, and squeeze whatever enjoyment you can out of it.

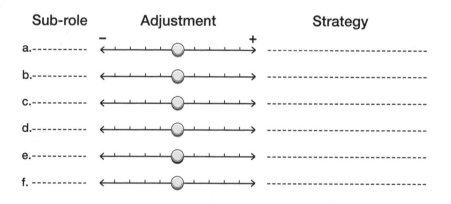

The Calm Way: Simplify.

Life editing

If you're making a movie or writing a book, one of the critical stages of transforming the raw material into a powerful finished product is editing. This is where you remove unnecessary material—taking 10 minutes of film and trimming it to two 10-second scenes—so that you end up with a scene that communicates faster and more meaningfully than the original footage.

The same can apply to your life.

Once you've looked at how you'd like to rebalance your life roles, and thought through the strategies of how you're going to do it, you may come to the conclusion that there's just too much "raw material." Too many things going on in your life. Too much work and unfinished business. Too many home duties, responsibilities, and ambitions. Too many feelings and sensitivities of other people that you have to contend with. Too many *things* cluttering up your life.

All this *stuff*, or clutter, or disorder, weighs heavily. It sucks your energy, adds to your responsibilities, and makes it difficult for you to focus on the things that are important. Clearing out the clutter—mental as well as physical—is a great way to start restoring harmony and balance.

In this chapter we're going to explore a range of ways you can reduce the clutter in your life. So that you can do this in a constructive way and never lose sight of what's important or what is dispensable, keep your Balance Vision handy.

A clean start

Physical clutter is the easy part. You can see it, touch it, reorder it. It would be a good start if you could reorder part of it right now.

Yes, right now. No matter how minor or trivial it may seem, start to bring some semblance of order to your immediate domain—your desk, your bedside table, your living room—so that there is visible evidence that the change has begun. Close this book for a moment and take some sort of reordering step now. Any step.

How did that feel? Isn't it refreshing to discover that even such simple actions can have a cleansing, energizing effect?

Now, while you're on a roll, let's start removing some of the physical clutter in other parts of your life.

- Your filing. Sort it into four stacks—"vital," "important," "things I'll get to later," and "trash." Throw out the last two.
- Your wardrobe. All those garments you've been saving until you trimmed down a bit can go. All those fashions and colors you thought were going to come back can go. Same with the shoes, belts, jumpers, coats, and baseball caps—just keep the ones that make you feel good when you put them on, and say good-bye to the rest. There are thousands of needy people and charities waiting—right now—for treasures such as these.
- Your books and recordings. Be harsh. Toss the ones you're not reading or are never going to. Yes, it may be true that intelligent, scholarly people have bookcases full of books, but it's also true that bookcases full of books will not make you intelligent or scholarly. Forget all that elitist sentiment about the glory of the printed word, and pass the books on to someone who'll *read* them. Books and CDs are as dispensable as any other commodity.
- Your home. Yes, even your living space needs editing. If you were an efficiency expert brought in to sort out your house, what would you keep? What would you lose?
- Your office or workplace. How many staplers can you use in a lifetime? Floppy disks—throw them out.
- You're on a roll. Keep it up. What about all those unused appli-

ances? The spare parts for your camera or computer? All those different shades of makeup you'll never wear again? The spare suitcase you bought to bring back more clutter from your last vacation? The paintings, the exercise bike, the special wine-glasses, the dumbbells, the ski jacket, the stamp collection, the novelties, the childhood trinkets that you're never going to use or look at again . . .

Whatever you think you could live without, and that could provide joy or value to someone else, should be on your toss list. Be brave. Be bold. You'll feel over the moon when you've done it. (Just keep checking your Balance Vision to ensure that you don't get too carried away.)

And while you're in the mood for recycling stuff, here are a few common excuses you can discard.

"I might need it one day." You won't. But there may be someone else who does. Check out the charities, and put it to good use.

"You wouldn't believe what I paid for that!" We would. But that was an investment in your past enjoyment—not in perfect balance. Think of it as you'd think of a great vacation: been there, done that, created a fond memory.

"It's part of me." It's part of the *old* you. The new, uncluttered, well-balanced you may not be so dependent on it.

Editing your habits

Clearing the clutter in your physical world is a piece of cake. "How badly do I want to keep this? Should I let it go? Next!"

This next part of the equation is a touch more challenging. It's to do with editing your habits and wasteful routines.

Every part of your life is dictated by habits or unconscious routines. In most cases, you never think about them. Yet they could be limiting your ability to enjoy or find balance in life. Why? Because they can blind you to more effective or efficient ways of doing things.

Once they've been identified, most habits can be modified by consciously taking a different approach. To edit the more ingrained ones involves four steps.

1. Identify the habit.
2. Identify how it's trying to help you (the reason it exists).
3. Find a more creative way to do it.
4. Fill the gap that is left.

IDENTIFY THE HABIT. You probably think this is the easy part. While it may be easy to recognize obvious habits such as smoking, overeating, and biting your fingernails, you'll have a harder time seeing the more routine ones, which can be even more limiting.

If you analyze all the different things you did last week, you'll discover a range of reflex activities that you hardly ever notice or think about. Many of these resulted in significant interruptions to your day but accounted for very little gain.

Why do you print and manually file your e-mails? Why do you wait till the last minute in the morning before you iron your shirt for work? Why do you take calls from unidentified salesmen at any hour of the day? Why do you fill out all the sections on your order-request forms when nobody reads past the first box? Why do you have eight columns on your spreadsheet when your accountant requires only three?

Many of these regular activities are little more than habits or routines that may have been important once but no longer make sense. If they stand in the way of or don't support your Balance Vision, they can be edited.

IDENTIFY HOW IT'S TRYING TO HELP YOU. Habits usually develop for what your subconscious perceives as a good reason. You don't overeat because you want to put on weight; you do so because you subconsciously believe your body needs extra fuel. You don't smoke because you enjoy the health risk; you do so because your subconscious is convinced you're a smoker. (And what's the one thing a smoker does? Exactly.) Or because your subconscious is convinced smoking will soothe your nerves.

And you don't work late each evening because you want to stay away from your family; you do so because you subconsciously believe this is the only way you can perform to the level expected of you.

FIND A MORE CREATIVE WAY TO DO IT. Your subconscious encourages you to do something habitually because it believes this is in your best interest. Even if you consciously decide to adopt a more favorable practice, your subconscious will not give up easily. It will continue to make its presence felt until you've found a way of removing the underlying "reason" for the habit, or you've found a more acceptable way of dealing with it.

Even though you habitually work late for flawed reasons, you subconsciously believe this is the best way. The only way of overcoming this limiting belief is to find a positive, acceptable alternative. This could be to create a *new* habit of, say, leaving work on time at least three days a week.

FILL THE GAP THAT IS LEFT. Sometimes when you have removed a habit or changed a belief, there is a "gap" left in your inner life. If this gap is not filled, you could find other, less desirable habits building or the old ones reemerging.

If you were to remove a smoking habit, for example, a number of gaps arise. What do you do with your hands? What do you do after meals? What do you do while you're standing around with a drink in your hand at a party? In each of these instances, you would need to find a creative way to fill the gap that is left. Now's a good time to start making a list of these unwanted habits, and some ways to fill the gaps once they're gone.

Editing your roles

Okay, you're getting the hang of this editing business.

The next step relates to editing your roles. You've already come part of the way here when you adjusted the emphasis of each role with your sliding scale device and when you formulated strategies for achieving this. Now we're going to go a step further and question some of these roles altogether. As with other methods in this book, there's a hard way to do this and there's the Calm Way.

The Calm Way begins with your Balance Vision, which sets the tone and direction for what follows.

> The Calm Way to edit your baggage: Once you have a clear idea of where you're heading, it's not hard to decide what to take with you.

If you take the four charts of your roles and compare them with your Balance Vision, you'll find that some roles fit neatly with it, while others seem to have no relevance whatsoever.

Assess each of your roles now. Be honest: Do they fit with the kind of life you described in your Balance Vision? Do they support it? Will they help you realize this ideal?

Make these evaluations as fluidly as you can. Follow your intuition and, for the moment, forget about your likes or the ramifications of each role.

Now that you've identified the roles that don't support your Balance Vision, you have to deal with them, either through elimination or relegation.

Some roles are harder to discard or downplay than others. Your Work roles may not allow you a lot of room to move; after all, your boss probably won't be all that impressed if you announce, "I don't do account summaries anymore." Similarly, when you consider your family roles, you may find there's not a lot that you *want* to toss out; on the contrary, your Social roles are usually the ones you want to add to, not reduce.

That leaves the roles that are discretionary and under your personal control. Often these are the roles you enjoy most. Are you meant to give them up? If you love dancing and do it every opportunity you can, you certainly wouldn't want to eliminate something that gives you so much pleasure. Even if it doesn't feature on your Balance Vision, it could still be an essential recreational part of maintaining a balanced life for you. On the other hand, if it keeps you out late every night at clubs and leaves you feeling drained in the mornings, it needs review.

Culling the "gonnas"

As you sort through the clutter in your life, you may find that its most pressing parts are not the things you're doing but the things you're not doing: the "should haves," the "have tos," and the "gonnas."

I *should have* volunteered for the fundraising committee. One day *I have to* finish my MBA. Someday *I'm gonna* learn tae kwon do and become a super-fit martial artist.

Should haves, have tos, and gonnas are nagging reminders of how much you have on your plate, or how much you still haven't done. So now is the perfect opportunity to clear the decks. First, ask yourself, "What's the worst that could happen if I don't do these?" Then, be tough: get rid of everything you're never really going to complete.

There, don't you feel better?

Even with the best of intentions, you're bound to find one or two roles that refuse to be brushed aside. But at least now you only have to focus on one or two rather than many.

Downscaling

No doubt you've come across the topic of "downscaling" or "downshifting" or "voluntary simplicity" in recent times. It's about reducing consumption, turning your back on materialism, and returning to the old-fashioned values of simplicity and frugality.

The appeal of downsizing is immediate to anyone who is enduring great job stress. The idea of being able to quit one's job and take off to the countryside for a carefree life of tending pumpkins, baking bread, and spending long hours by the fireside has crossed many a tense executive's mind. Some have succumbed to it. Interestingly, this has been a fantasized-about ideal since the time of Socrates.

However, I have observed a similarity of experience in many of those who've made such transitions. They find themselves either taking their driven urban habits to more relaxed environs where they end up re-creating their old worlds (often quite successfully) or becoming disenchanted with their new worlds after a couple of years and then returning to their original.

What this suggests is that a changed environment or downscaling is not much of a solution if the problem is your own frame of mind. If you can't find a way to be happy where you're living now, you may find you're no happier if you shift somewhere else. If you can't find a way to be happy with a Mercedes-Benz in your garage, you probably won't be any happier if you downsize to a Toyota.

Naturally, this doesn't apply to every person and every situation. But it does highlight the difference between real simplification and romantic idealism. The way I see it, the romantic approach is little more than "I'll get more enjoyment out of that lifestyle than this one." On the other hand, simplification is a profound way to get rid of distraction and trim your life down to its richest components.

> The Calm Way: Happiness doesn't depend on what you have but how you feel about what you have. With a minimum of effort, you can change the way you feel about most things.

We'll now explore the principles that underpin the concept of simplification, or life editing.

- **Shed the stuff that slows you down.**
  Getting rid of things just for the sake of getting rid of them doesn't make a whole lot of sense. But it does make sense to get rid of things—ideas and beliefs as much as the possessions—that lock you in a place you don't want to be.

  There is a direct link between materialism and stress. The more you pursue worldly success, the more you strive to attain, the more stress you feel. The more you have, the more you think you need. The higher you go, the more emotionally bound you become to your "successes."

It's not unusual to feel a great sense of relief when you step away from this. Providing that you do it purposefully and constructively, shedding some of this clutter can be very liberating.

- **Always trade up; never trade down.**
  At first, this sentiment may appear counterintuitive. Most people consider the concept of downscaling as a way of reducing the value of what they have rather than increasing it.

  But the variable here is what is meant by "value." If you interpret value as a measure of how something improves your life, then "trading up" is a simple principle to accept, even if you are seeking a less materialistic way of life.

  Once you can see your moves in this light, you see how it becomes possible to "trade up" to a cheaper car or an older car, or even no car at all—as long as you feel that such a move adds value to your life. Then you can refocus your efforts on lifting your *quality* of living rather than your standard of living. Focus on a life that is outwardly more simple yet inwardly more satisfying and rich.

- **Understand the difference between stimulation and simple pleasures.**
  On page 113 you saw the two contrasting sides of the human nervous system. One side responds to excitement and tends to seek more and more stimulation. The other side tries to restore the equilibrium by helping you relax. Ideally, your daily life will fluctuate between these two states, stimulation and relaxation.

  Unfortunately, today's emphasis is on stimulation. We try to squeeze more and more of it into our day. And it's got to the stage where most people now rely on some form of stimulation in an effort to relax. Unfortunately, your nervous system doesn't work like this. Stimulation is the opposite of relaxation. Stimulation is designed to arouse the senses and nervous system, while relaxation is designed to soothe them. Once you recognize stimulation for what it is—the radio that wakes you, the espresso at breakfast, the newspaper on the train, the animated screen saver at work, the spicy food at lunch, the sugar hit in the afternoon, the cop show at night—you see how all-pervasive it has become.

There's nothing wrong with stimulation and excitement; it's just that they're not relaxation. And often they lead you to overlook the simple, less dynamic pleasures of life. The early morning sunrise. The peaceful look on your sleeping daughter's face. A cool, crisp sugar-snap pea. The gaze of an adoring pet. The sound of a soft breeze rustling through poplars.

Recognizing the difference between these extremes—stimulation and simple, relaxed pleasures—is a vital step in simplifying your life.

- **Pay attention to what you really want.**
  One of the by-products of consumerism is that it encourages us to link real human needs (physical, social, psychological, spiritual) with the production and consumption of man-made goods and services.

  Regardless of how impervious we think we are to this, most of us have spent many years in consumer training. We've been conditioned to want things long before we have the need for them. You see a new imported foodstuff in the supermarket, and you start imagining how you could incorporate it into your menu this week. You see a new gadget on television, and you start thinking of how it could be useful to you. You read about a new book promising a perfectly balanced life, and you immediately think you've been waiting for this since you first started working. You hear about a fancy new shampoo that makes the ends of your hair flick upward, and you convince yourself you've always wished someone was going to invent such a shampoo. Most of these are retrospective needs, sometimes created by you but usually by the marketing departments of the manufacturers.

Resisting these "needs" requires more effort than you might think. Why? First, because your "I'm resisting consumerism" inclinations are easily exploited by alert marketers. (Who thought up all those no-packaging, no-brand-name, eco-friendly, generic, no-frills, nonadvertised, consumer-refillable products?) Second, because the quest for novelty is a very human trait.

If you want to simplify your life, pay close attention to your real needs—long before you think about shopping—and let everything else go.

- **Develop new status symbols.**
  In a perfect world, status symbols would not be important to us. But we're not perfect, we do have egos, and we do like to have people think we're beautiful, accomplished, sexy, sophisticated, intelligent, spiritual, nonconsumerist—whatever. Status symbols are a shortcut to these impressions.

  Status symbols don't just happen. Most are created by people in marketing departments, who are delighted when you accept their recommendations as to what will improve your perceived status in life. But they're not the only ones who can create status symbols. You can create your own. How about this, for example:

  My status is confirmed by the fact that I am a happy and contented person.

  Or:

  My status is confirmed by the fact that I have lots of time to spend with my friends and family.

- **Spend less than you earn.**
  It sounds obvious, doesn't it? Even though it was the first rule of commerce we all learned, it's the first one people tend to forget. Easy credit has meant that many of us now spend more than we earn in the belief that it will all work out in the days ahead—when we'll be earning more, or when asset growth has made up for the debt, or who-knows-what other theory.

  Yet, whatever you borrow, you have to repay. Regardless of the wisdom of using other people's money to build wealth or enhance your lifestyle now, debt adds pressure. At least it does for most people. So, if you're one of those people, and you want to simplify, move toward clearing your debts.

- **Know when to call it a day.**
  This is the greatest dilemma of all—knowing when enough is enough, at least from a material perspective. At what stage do you say, "I've gone as far up the ladder as I need to; now I'm going to ease off"? Or, "I have enough possessions to last me three lifetimes; I'm opting out of the consuming race." Or, "I'll soon own my own home, the children's education has been paid for, I'm going to take it easier from now on." At what stage does the struggle end?

  If you really are battling to meet your daily needs, this is easy to answer. But the more affluent you become, the harder it is to resolve. You see this illustrated time and time again in sociological studies when the question is posed, "Can you afford all you really need in life?" On average, the more affluent the respondent (up to a point), the more often you get a "No" response.

  So how do you avoid this? How do you see through the illusions of affluence and really get to the truth of what you need? Easy. Refer to your Balance Vision and establish clear strategies on how you're going to realize it.

- **Learn to live with purpose.**

  The most overlooked but possibly the most important aspect of "downscaling" is its underlying philosophy: the objective is not so much to learn to live with less as to learn to live more deliberately and purposefully—growing as an individual, enriching your community and planet. In other words, to live a more fulfilling and balanced life.

  As long as you approach this with positive intentions and appreciate that there is a big difference between modesty and deprivation, you're headed in the right direction. Whether you ultimately get by with one car rather than two, with three bedrooms rather than four, with sensible working hours rather than a massive salary, with durable clothes rather than the latest fashion, with fresh produce rather than imported delicatessen items, is just a matter of scale and choice.

  Your choice.

Finally, an important note on perspective when it comes to life editing. We can all rail against overconsumption and consumerism, and sing the praises of modesty and moderation, but this sentiment applies differently to different people.

It's easy to see how a successful fifty-five-year-old stockbroker might consider downscaling and working only three days a week in his quest for a balanced, comfortable life. But this could be a meaningless fantasy to someone who can hardly get three days' work a week to start with.

It's easy to see how a stay-at-home mother might eschew packaged goods and supermarket items in favor of home-baked breads and organic vegetables. But this might be the last thing you'd consider if you were a single working parent who couldn't find adequate childcare and who didn't have time for shopping.

And it's easy to see how a person with a hou'
appliances might consider trading it all in for
wood fire. But this might seem alien and irr(
has toiled for years to afford a deposit on a small a.....
partner and children.

It's all a matter of perspective. And choice.

Your choice.

Clear out the clutter

One last thought on the topic of "heads." It's to do with mental clutter.

Mental clutter occurs when you can't concentrate, when your thoughts flit from one thing to another, and when you're feeling stressed, anxious, or overexcited. Like any other form of clutter, mental clutter makes it difficult for you to maintain balance in life.

Fortunately, it's fairly easy to reverse.

You've probably done this yourself in the past—after a few days on a relaxing vacation you notice how your thinking seems clearer, work problems seem smaller, thoughts seem more orderly, and new ideas spring to mind.

Although you can't remain on vacation forever, you can extend that feeling indefinitely. You can do this through regular meditation practice or through a combination of simple relaxation approaches, such as "Time to rebalance" (page 254) or "Deep Calm" (page 256).

Whether you use it to eliminate mental clutter or for other reasons, meditation is a wonderful way to add more balance to your life. If you can find a way to do it daily, you'll find that, after a time, perfect balance begins to occur without your doing a thing. I urge you to try it.

Hearts

There are three primary ways to adjust your life roles:
you make physical changes, you make attitudinal
changes, or other people make the changes.

You've taken the practical steps: you've developed strategies that
will help you balance your roles, and you've considered ways to edit
some of the more superfluous aspects of your life.

Now we're going to move into more powerful territory and
concentrate on what's in your heart: the emotional, intuitive, or
psychological ways that will help you find perfect balance. Why
more powerful? Because perfect balance is more a state of mind than
a state of affairs, and these are the ways you influence your state of
mind. To do this, you may have to challenge your current perspectives and boundaries.

Perspectives

You can turn your life around—bad into good, humdrum into inspiring, meaningless into meaningful—with small shifts of perspective.

Have you ever noticed how two people can view exactly the same
event and form opposite impressions? One sees a roller-coaster as
fun and stimulating; the other sees it as frightening and dangerous.
One sees an argumentative client as interesting and involving; the
other sees him as rude and threatening. One sees a huge workload as

a sign of interest and usefulness; the other sees it as oppressive and stressful. One sees long work hours as an unwelcome intrusion on her life; the other sees them as a refuge from what awaits at home, such as marriage or financial problems.

In a perfect world you could change your perspective at any time to suit your requirements or eliminate the patterns and beliefs that hold you back. But if you attempt this the hard way and try to *force* yourself to change, you don't have a hope.

> The Calm Way: The most effective way to consciously change a thought or stream of thinking is to consciously substitute another for it.

The Calm Way is more effective. It recognizes that your perspective on events is not a psychological fixture—it can be modified. We're not talking about major attitudinal overhauls here or curing phobias or compulsions. All we're concerned with is a subtle recoloring of everyday events such as your job, your workload, and the amount of time you have at your disposal. There are simple tools that will help you do this.

- **Choice**
  Making a conscious choice to adopt one frame of mind in preference to another is something any person can do. You can change your perspectives, the way you think, what you believe, and how you behave; you can even change lifelong habits. But the first step is making the decision, actually choosing to do it.

- **Imagination**
  Your imagination is the main tool of your subconscious. As such, it can be more motivating and compelling than any amount of information or knowledge.

For example, you can have a dozen experts *prove* that you're much better off working more hours each day, but it won't mean a thing if you *imagine* that your boss is trying to take advantage of your good nature. Similarly, you can have a truckload of statistics that show people never fall when they walk across narrow wooden planks, but if a plank is stretched between two skyscrapers, your imagination will prevent you from taking a step. Knowledge is no match for what you imagine.

It's easy to make your imagination work to your advantage. If you can imagine what it will be like when you've achieved a certain goal, it will be markedly easier to realize. The more detail you can apply to this—the look on your face, how you'll be feeling, the sounds you'll be hearing, the "shape and texture" of the results—the more achievable your goals become.

- **Substitution**

Despite what you think, you have no conscious control over your thoughts. No amount of willpower or intellectual effort can make them behave the way you tell them to. The only way you can consciously change a thought or stream of thinking is to consciously substitute another for it.

You cannot consciously force yourself not to think of the unpleasant news your accountant just gave you, but you can stop thinking about it by substituting another thought: what you're going to prepare for dinner tonight.

This means you can overcome negative feelings or impressions by substituting them with positive ones. Instead of concentrating on the hours you still have to work, concentrate on how much you're enjoying what you're doing at this moment. You can also use substitution in a more concrete way: instead of struggling to reduce your travel time, find ways to use your travel time productively. And so on.

As an agent for change, substitution is much more powerful than brute willpower.

- **Emotion**

As with what you imagine, what you feel about an issue is more influential than what you know about it.

Knowledge or information amounts to very little if there is no feeling that accompanies it; you probably won't even remember the information. So if you want to change any aspect of your life, your attitudes or perspectives, don't hold back—add emotion to it. When there's a strong emotion attached, even the most trivial piece of knowledge can produce change.

- **Focus**

To a large extent, the life you live is prejudiced by the parts of it that you pay attention to.

If you go to work tomorrow and focus on the walls that need painting, the overdraft that's growing, and all the work you need to catch up on, you'll have a pretty miserable job.

But if you go to work tomorrow and see a brilliant poster instead of a scruffy wall, a raft of forward bookings instead of the overdraft, and a string of accomplishments you'd managed throughout the year instead of how much work you still have to do, you'll believe you have a much better job than in that first instance. Exactly the same job, but two completely different impressions of it.

This is the power of focus. If you focus on the good things in your life, you continually find good things taking place. If you focus on beauty, you see beauty everywhere. If you associate with happy people, you will feel happier.

And if you concentrate on the balanced and harmonious parts of your life, all the other parts of it will seem more balanced and harmonious.

> The Calm Way: Highlight the balanced and harmonious aspects of your life, and the rest of it will seem more balanced and harmonious.

- **Repetition**

What's the single greatest influence on your attitudes, beliefs, capabilities, and emotions? Repetition. Whether it comes from the words you mentally say to yourself or the actions you perform, repetition is the key to learning and change.

You can use it to rearrange the importance of events or pressures. "I'm really enjoying this task, I'm really enjoying this task, I'm really enjoying this task"—even if you were to say this on the most superficial level, you'd begin to view the task differently. Hard to accept but easily proved. Any comment or thought repeated often enough becomes ingrained in your consciousness and soon begins to direct your thinking and actions.

When you have decided on the goals you will pursue, any form of repetition—mental rehearsal, repeated verbalizing, or viewing in written form—will make them more attainable.

Time in perspective

Because "time pressure" is the most cited cause of stress in today's workplace, it's worth singling out a Calm Way of getting it into perspective.

About a century ago the expert on time, Albert Einstein, wrote that "the distinction between the past, the present and the future is only an illusion." If you accept that, it doesn't take much effort to work out that time cannot exert pressure because it has no substance. If pressure exists, it's because of your attitude toward time or your perception of it. Which is just as well, because time can't be changed, whereas attitudes and perceptions can.

On the very simplest level, you can start to soften your attitudes and perceptions of time right now. If you're like millions of others in the workplace, you'll have an annoying little voice in your head that consistently warns you of how little time you have. "I have to hurry." "There's no time for . . ." "I'm running out of time." And whether this chatter is going on consciously or unconsciously, it adds to the pressure you might be feeling. Internal dialogue has a potent psychological effect; it's one of the main drivers of how you feel at any given moment.

There is a Calm Way to reverse the feelings of pressure that internal dialogue creates. You simply substitute positive internal chatter to counteract the negative. When people complete our courses, they usually end up with a more friendly and accommodating voice in their consciousness; instead of constantly hearing how little time they have, they're hearing that they have "all the time in the world."

This change is achieved through a simple affirmation technique. Don't be deceived by its simplicity; this is a serious psychological tool used by psychotherapists and hypnotherapists the world over. Known as self-instruction or auto-suggestion, it derives its power from unthinking repetition. As the repeated words implant themselves in your subconscious, they become self-fulfilling. Try it. You'll be surprised how quickly it starts to work.

- Choose a set of positive words that sum up how you'd like to be feeling. This sentiment could even be the opposite of what you've been subconsciously telling yourself. The expression

I like to use for myself is "I have all the time in the world," but you may think of something more appropriate to your circumstances.

- To bring it into reality, all you have to do is repeat those words. Over and over. Silently. Loudly if you wish. Dozens or even hundreds of times a day. The more you repeat them, the more they counter the internal dialogue that makes you feel under pressure.
- Once you've done this a few times, you start to feel that time pressure is not as threatening as it was. You start to feel that you have more time to do things. And the more you repeat those words, the more relaxed about time you begin to feel.

To help you get time into a more manageable perspective, use "The moment is now" on page 243.

Boundaries

Throughout this book I've been urging you to take a holistic approach toward finding perfect balance. Once you do this, all parts will be seamlessly interlinked and supportive of one another. From a holistic perspective, there are no boundaries: whether you're working, playing, loving, meditating, or studying, everything links and blends.

Unfortunately, there are aspects of today's working world that stand in the way of this ideal.

- Many employers believe that the intrusiveness of an employee's personal life reduces their productivity.
- Many employees (or self-employed) believe the intrusiveness of work responsibilities limits their ability to enjoy their personal life.

- And many of those in between, usually family members or friends, believe their world suffers when either of the above boundaries is breached too often.

This imbalance is usually weighted in the employer's favor because they do a better job of keeping personal issues out of the workplace than employees do at keeping work issues out of their personal lives.

So from a simple management point of view, we may need to constantly remind ourselves where one part of our world ends and another begins. This is not as easy as it used to be. We live in an age where boundaries are increasingly blurred. Today you can work from home as easily as from the office. You can communicate with your child in the classroom. Your colleagues can reach you any time, any place. You can check sporting results, trade shares, or edit a movie from a rowboat. You can collaborate on a transnational document without giving a second thought to the difference in time

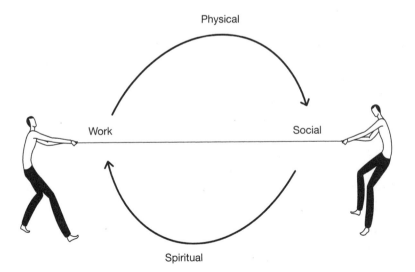

zones. With the advent of mobile technology—laptops, phones, e-mail, Internet, streaming video—not only is it easy for your worlds to overlap, it is almost impossible to avoid. When this overlap exists, problems arise.

Some people find that blurred boundaries lead to a cycle of tension: pressure at work causes you to feel physically and emotionally stressed; you take these feelings home and they cause problems in your personal life; the tension in your home life makes you question the worth of what you do for a living (Spiritual); this doubt carries over to your next working day and causes you to perform below expectation, which adds to your feeling of pressure at work . . . and so the cycle continues.

Others find that blurred boundaries limit their efficiency. Contrary to all boasts and ideals about multitasking, most people can't manage it on a sustained basis. For those who do manage it, there's a price to pay—usually in relation to physical and mental health, possibly relationships as well.

So, with a holistic ideal of perfect balance in mind, you may need to formalize some of the boundaries between your work and personal life.

Defining the boundaries

For some fortunate people, life is just one big party. They approach everything with the same zest—work, play, relationships—without consideration of where one part ends and another begins.

Others go through life with a much clearer sense of where the boundaries exist. They're the ones who deal with all kinds of work loads and pressures throughout the workday, then the minute they finish work, they immediately slip into a more casual frame of mind.

And others, especially high achievers, live with a constant work-home overlap.

What about you? Where do you fit?

If you find yourself chewing over work issues while you're dining with your partner, or being unable to help your daughter with her homework because you have a briefcase full of documents to review tonight, you probably need to formalize the boundaries between work and home.

Conversely, if you find it frustrating and distracting to have your mother calling your office every half hour for advice on wallpaper colors, you probably need to formalize the boundaries between home and work.

In both cases there is a physical separation that can make this task easier. Far more challenging is where there's no strict physical delineation between your two worlds—such as when you work from home, or run a family business, or don't work fixed hours. In these instances, you may need to create your own physical or psychological boundaries.

Physical boundaries

Most people who work at a place other than home have a clear separation of their work and home environments. They leave one zone and they enter another; they leave one frame of mind and they come home to another.

If you're a telecommuter, or self-employed, or work from home, this is not always possible. However, even if both occur under one roof, you can still distinguish between work and family spaces. The obvious way is to have a room dedicated as your workspace. If this can't be achieved, you can nominate a specific area for this purpose, such as one end of the dining table.

You can increase this sense of partition by nominating specific work hours and being disciplined about keeping them. "Between eight and four every day I work on my book. All domestic issues are on hold until after this time." Then, to define the division even more, you can reserve certain equipment and accessories (pens, filing cabinets, telephones) for work time, not to be used during home time.

After a while, this separation will help you build a psychological boundary between the two contesting parts of your life.

Psychological boundaries

Physical boundaries require effort, but they are easy to live with. Mental and behavioral boundaries are easier to create, but they require more discipline to maintain.

Anything that causes you to stop thinking "work" and start thinking "home" will have the desired effect. Even simple things like changing clothes will do.

The surest way to establish psychological boundaries is the principle of finishing your work at work. Once you leave your workplace, whether it is in another suburb or at the other end of your dining table, that's it for working for the day. If you are unwavering about this and make the switch-off point the moment you leave, you'll find it becomes second nature.

Why stop thinking about work at your workplace rather than when you arrive home? Why not use your travel time for working through unresolved work on your way home?

If your mind is filled with work on the way home, and vice versa on your way to work, you'll arrive at one destination in the other's frame of mind. It then takes some time to readjust, which could lead to the kind of tensions you're trying to avoid. Better to arrive home in a "home" frame of mind (or at least not in a work frame of mind). You can reverse this the following day, when you resume thinking of work the moment you walk out the front door in the morning—if that's what you want.

One final note of comfort: all this information about establishing boundaries is relevant only when you're working toward perfect balance. Once you have arrived at the state where *you feel your life is perfectly balanced,* boundaries become increasingly unimportant because you will have developed a holistic perspective on life and its many components.

Clocks

There are three primary ways to adjust your life roles: you make physical changes, you make attitudinal changes, or other people make the changes.

As we've seen, you can adjust the balance between most of the pressures in your life through practical as well as psychological measures.

The topic of time could have been handled in such a way. But because it impacts on almost every person's view of their life balance, we'll consider time in its own right.

Your attitudes toward time are a factor of the age in which you live. The world is getting busier: workloads seem to be increasing in inverse proportion to deadlines, and social (family, home, friends) demands seem to be increasing in inverse proportion to the time we have available to satisfy them. In other words, our work and social responsibilities are growing as our available time is shrinking.

Is it any wonder that we believe there is always more we have to accomplish in the time we have available? Or that there is never enough time to accomplish all we have to do? Adding to this is the psychological phenomenon that the more stressed we feel, the less time we believe we have. As a result, society has invented a wonderful new burden for us to contend with: "time pressure."

You can deal with this in two different ways: psychologically or tactically; either use the "Hearts" adjustment mode from the previous section or concentrate on scheduling. You cannot deal with stress and a feeling of lack of time through time management! Time is nothing more than the interval between two events, so it can only be measured, not managed. All you can hope to manage is your attitude toward time, and the things you do or schedule within a specific period.

Scheduling has its limits: if your starting point is a full agenda, you can't just add activities as you think of them. To increase the time for one activity (such as home life), you have to reduce the time you allow for another (such as work). This is not always possible.

The Calm Way takes a more holistic approach. Instead of trying to micromanage schedules, the Calm Way rebalances the weightings between roles. This is achieved through ranking, budgeting, and doubling, which we will discuss now.

> The Calm Way: Balance has more to do with what your thoughts say than what your clock says.

Ranking

Among life's many inevitabilities are three that relate to time.
- Most time is spent on your least rewarding activities.
- The most important tasks and activities usually give way to the most pressing.
- The most pressing are seldom the most important.

Or are these inevitable?

With a modicum of effort you can ensure that the most important parts of your life get the attention they deserve. The secret to doing this is ranking: determining what is most important, then concentrating on these first.

How ranking works

You probably believe you have a finite amount of time to devote to your different interests and responsibilities. This means you can accommodate some of them with satisfaction and peace of mind or all of them with no satisfaction at all.

Assuming that you chose satisfaction and peace of mind, which activities are you prepared to forego or compromise on? Here's how to make the decision.
- Use the following table to make a list of all the activities that take up your time during the day and evening. There should be about 20 or so items on this list. Maybe more.

ACTIVITY	A	B	C	D

- Rate each activity on your list according to the following measures:
  A = Absolutely essential
  B = Desirable, and I love doing it
  C = Desirable
  D = I could get by without this
- Now cross out every activity that you've rated C or D. From now on, we're going to concentrate on the activities you've rated A or B, and ignore the rest.

What you've managed to do with this exercise is to rank the activities that take up your time. A few minutes ago, they all seemed important in one way or another. Now you have a list of those that really deserve your attention. Focus on these. Be disciplined.

Budgeting

In my earlier book, *Calm at Work*, we introduced the concept of time allocation as a way of dealing with perceived time pressures. In recent years, some of the businesspeople I've worked with have taken this a step further. They've introduced the concept of "time budgeting"—a relationship that is much more meaningful to business.

From their management point of view, time is a finite resource that's every bit as valuable and measurable as labor and money. In the context of a working year, they have a specific number of hours to invest in a specific number of tasks—big-picture tasks such as making a successful business and detailed tasks such as mailing out the invoices each week. The hours required to fulfill each of these tasks are allocated accordingly. This is where the notion of time budgeting arises.

This is not the first time you've encountered the relationship between time and finance. You "buy some time," "spend some time," and "save time." You may even say outright that "time is money." So budgeting time should be an easy concept to work with.

We can learn a lot from this business perspective. If you apply this thinking to your life, you'll do away with much of what you now see as time pressure. True, it may persist at the micro level, such as when you have to complete a certain project by a certain hour, but it will be eliminated as a generalized, overriding pressure.

The starting point for time budgeting is acknowledging that you can't "spend" more hours than you have in total. If you spend too much in one area, you must economize in another—a principle you're familiar with in your day-to-day financial budgeting. This means that you have to limit the number or the duration of your activities to fit the time you have allowed. Alternatively, you need to seek a greater time allocation (such as from your boss, your professor, your client, or your publisher).

Once you have accepted this principle, there are two simple steps to follow.

> The Calm Way: Budgeting your time does not remove the spontaneity from your life. It creates the opportunity for spontaneity.

Step 1: Use your calendar before your diary
Taking a holistic view of your life means looking at it from a long-term perspective. What is your total time budget? Five years? That's 60 months, 260 weeks, 1826 days.

- **Budget for "once-in-a-lifetime" events**
  If you want to travel to Japan sometime in the next five years,

allocate some of that time for it now. Go ahead and schedule it (you can always change the date). In this way, it ceases to be a "Someday I have to" event and becomes a real fixture. One pressure removed.

- **Budget for your vacations**
  Next, schedule your vacations. Ideally, one per year. A total allocation of, say, 100 days from your time budget.

- **Budget for important events**
  Allocate some of your budget to the bigger events you'd like to fit into your year—your friend's wedding, the managing-customer-relations course, your son's graduation, your quarterly weekend retreat. Schedule them in. As time rolls on, you will think of others; you can fit these in, too, if your budget permits.

Step 2: Now use your diary

Once your calendar features the more important events of your work and personal life, you can work around these for the remainder of your schedule.

First, allocate time for yourself.

- **Budget your weekends**
  If you've tended to think of your diary as being a tool for your workday, now's the time to adjust that point of view and start thinking of your life as a whole—workdays, evenings, and especially weekends.

- **Budget for "rebalancing"**
  Set aside a period of quiet time each day—20 to 30 minutes is best—that you designate "Time to rebalance" (page 254). Whether you use this time to meditate or sit in a warm bath is less important than the fact that you set it aside and use it.

- **Budget for your relationships**

  When you get caught up in the maelstrom of a busy week, it's easy to lose sight of the simple things that give you pleasure and enrich your life. Relationships, for example.

  If you want to spend more time with your partner and children during the week, now's the time to allocate some of your budget to it. Perhaps you could schedule in a date once a week. Or schedule in the time to read a story to your toddler each evening.

- **Budget for your health**

  It's easy to overlook the one thing that enables you to lead the busy life that you do: your health. While diet probably doesn't need any time provision, what about exercise? If you think it's important to go to the gym twice a week, allocate the time for it. Schedule it in.

- **Budget for your personal development**

  If there's a course you want to do or studies you want to undertake, now is the time to budget for them. Claim the time; schedule it.

- **Budget for your work duties**

  As well as budgeting for your routine work activities, put aside a certain amount of time *every day* for focusing on your own tasks and thinking time. Allow no meetings, phone calls, or interruptions during these times.

Making work the last item on your budgeting list doesn't mean it's less important than other activities in your life. It just means that you've put yourself first; you've started to consider your own needs as well as your duties.

Doubling

The dream of true multitasking is a product of the computer age. In principle, it's where a computer processor undertakes several tasks simultaneously. But what's good for your computer is not necessarily good for your mental well-being.

When multitasking migrated from computers to people—as some sort of industrial fantasy in which one person might perform the duties of several—it became more sinister. Consider some of the everyday tasks that people attempt at the same time.

Task A	Task B
Writing a document	Fielding calls from customers
Teaching the class	Correcting the term papers
Measuring the dosage	Checking the blood-pressure monitor
Driving a car	Using a mobile phone
Cooking dinner	Helping with homework
Filing the papers	Mentally compiling a to-do list
Compiling a spreadsheet	Preparing for a meeting

While it's easy to see the appeal of being able to perform two or more tasks simultaneously, it comes at a price. For a start, most people just can't do it for extended periods. Second, even if they could, they couldn't do it efficiently; in fact, there are several studies that show how multitasking reduces productivity rather than improves it. Third, even by attempting to do this, you create stress for yourself.

In spite of this, what I'm about to suggest here relates to doing two things at once. "Doubling," however, is different from the traditional way—the hard way, if you like—in that it's about doing one thing consciously and another mechanically.

For example, you can chew gum and type a letter at the same time. You do one thing consciously (typing) and another unconsciously (chewing). This is the principle that underpins doubling. Here are some ways you could apply it to your life.

- Determine what kinds of repetitive, unconscious (mechanical) activities exist in your day.
- Choose conscious activities that you can perform at the same time.
- Make sure the two activities are complementary in approach (such as traveling to work and planning your day).

Here are some examples where doubling may work.

Mechanical activity	Conscious activity
Commuting	Planning, working through issues
Bathing	Problem-solving
Exercising	Mental rehearsal for meeting
Cleaning	Compiling to-do list
Waiting for elevator	Planning for next task
Taking alone time	Meditation
Focusing on spiritual growth	Reading to children

If you find it difficult to fit in all you'd like to do in a given day, then doubling is a useful technique to consider. Like formalizing your work-home boundaries, doubling is a measure you employ on your way to perfect balance rather than after you've got there. When your life is perfectly balanced, you'll want to preserve as much as you can of your unconscious activity time as "free time"—space for daydreaming, meditating, or just logging out. Because, as I've said in other parts of this book, dividing your attention creates tension and unease, whereas focusing on only one thing is calming and fulfilling.

The hidden watch

Almost all time-focused people respond to one signal over and above all others: the signal from their wristwatch. You may think of yours as a fashion accessory or a useful tool for everyday life, but it can also be an intrusive source of negative energy. It makes its presence felt when you're under pressure, beckoning to you every few moments . . . ticking away, ticking away . . . reminding you of all you haven't done yet . . . ticking away, ticking away . . . keeping the pressure on.

Fortunately, there's an ingenious way to put time pressure in its place. It's a little trick you probably picked up yourself on vacation: You left your watch at home. (Or in your suitcase.)

You can bring back this carefree feeling now. Just by removing your watch. Try it now. Take it off and slip it into your pocket. After a while you will start to feel a subtle but real reminder that time is not so important. That's all you have to do. Try it. And be pleasantly surprised.

If you're normally a time-pressured person, you may feel a little apprehensive about this. "What if I miss my meeting?" "What if I'm late for my bus?"

One of the advantages of the hidden watch is that such mishaps seldom occur. For a start, you're surrounded by timepieces: your computer, your phone, on the coffee machine, on the DVD player, on your bedside table, on the wall—they're everywhere! Besides, there's a very accurate little clock inside you that will always remind you when it's a certain time, *as long as you have faith that it will do so.*

Take your watch off now. Slip it into your pocket. Trust your internal clock to remind you when your next engagement is due. And relish the carefree, pressure-free holiday feeling that such a simple gesture can create. There's no simpler demonstration that it's not time that creates the pressure but your attitude toward time.

Hiding your watch is one way to ease time pressure; knowing what's important—and prioritizing your activities—is another way. Other ways are budgeting, scheduling, and doubling.

Individually, each of these can help you adjust the weightings of your roles. Collectively, they are a great leap forward in achieving perfect balance.

> The Calm Way: If you can bring your attention back from the future and forward from the past, a perfectly balanced state exists at the point of intersection.

Negotiation

There are three primary ways to adjust your life roles:
you make physical changes, you make attitudinal changes,
or other people make the changes.

We've covered some of the ways you can adjust the balance between the roles via your own efforts. Now we come to a critical but much less predictable area: dealing with the needs and expectations of others.

It's possible that you could edit your roles, change your attitudes, and adjust your priorities, and then discover that your partner has other ideas completely. Or that your boss doesn't agree with any of it.

Confronted with others' expectations this way, you either have to go back to the drawing board or negotiate.

In the literal sense, negotiation is about reaching agreement through discussion and compromise. From this book's perspective, it means persuading others to accept the adjustments you've decided you want to make.

This is an important distinction. It's not about finding ways to be more accommodating of other people's needs and expectations; it's about persuasion.

Our approach to persuasion will focus on two steps: communicate and negotiate.

Once you've taken these steps, it's time to apply the N-word, which you'll read about later.

Communicate

When it comes to getting other people to agree with your rebalancing efforts, there is no substitution for communication. After all, what's the point in changing your calendar and diary to focus on your family needs and commitments, if key family members are planning something different? Or what's the point in planning a brilliant new approach to lessening your work hours, if your boss thinks you're not working hard enough as it is?

This is where communication and coordination come to the fore.

If other people are involved, your schedule and your needs have to dovetail with theirs. This means communication and being clear and precise about what you want.

This is only the start.

Communication is a two-way process. It only exists when the other party receives and understands what you intend. You cannot assume this has happened; you need a response. You cannot rely on your listener's sensitivity or intelligence; you must clearly state the response you require. "Can I assume that it's acceptable for me to vary my work hours this way?"

Then there's one more step: you must wait for the response.

> The Calm Way: Instead of waiting for an acceptable response,
> identify the response you find acceptable.

Negotiate

In a perfect world, you'd be able to tell someone what you wanted and they would agree or disagree according to whether the request was acceptable to them. Unfortunately, it's not a perfect world.

Whenever you want somebody else to accept your requests or to go along with changes you suggest, communication takes on a new complexity. Having a few negotiation skills will serve you well.

Generally, the approaches you use will depend on your relationship with the other party. These can range from problem-solving ("Let's see how we can find a solution"), to persuasion ("Do this, and it'll make you feel better"), to direct instruction ("Would you please do this"). Whatever approach you take, the steps you employ are the same.

- **Be clear about what you want to achieve**
  Amazingly, this is a step that's frequently overlooked. If you have a simple, clear idea of what you want to achieve from the negotiation, you start from a powerful position.

- **Point out the benefit**
  As you require the other person to respond to your proposal in some way, it must be in their interest to do so. They must emerge from the negotiation feeling they've benefited in some way by agreeing to your proposition. So think it through from their point of view. What's in it for them?

  If you simply ask, "Can I go home early today?" you'll get a "Why?" response. From that moment on, you're negotiating on the other party's terms. Not a good start.

  You will do much better with the standard "If . . . then" approach. "If you let me go home early today, then I will finish my work on Saturday." A condition followed by an offer.

- **Keep it positive**
Without exception, you have a better chance of getting your way if what you propose is framed in positive terms rather than negative. Hence, "Please help me finish this project" will always get you a better response than, "Please don't make me finish this by myself." In a similar vein, "Can you give me one more hour to do this?" will always get you a better response than, "Can you not give me so much to do?" Using simple, positive language is the most powerful way to negotiate.

- **Stick to the plot**
Children are very good at getting their own way. They have an effective, if sometimes irritating, habit of repeating the one simple request over and over. "Can I have more ice cream please? Can I have more ice cream please? Can I have more ice cream please?"

 If your request is clear and single-minded, you can be that persistent, too. This has many advantages, particularly when the negotiation strays into areas that don't serve your purpose. When this happens, you simply come back to the same old story.

 As blunt as this technique may seem, persistence and repetition have a way of paying off, especially if you know exactly what you want out of the negotiation.

- **Have an incentive up your sleeve**
If you've done your homework and worked out the most appealing benefit for the other party, your negotiation should be relatively straightforward—a bit of give and take, ending up with both parties feeling as if they've won in some way. However, there will be occasions when you'll need more incentive to get them over the line. This can take many forms, such as a contribution, concession, or compromise.

A **CONTRIBUTION**. What are you prepared to give in order to achieve your outcome? "If you let me go home at lunchtime today, then I will donate some of my day's salary to charity."

A **CONCESSION**. What are you prepared to forego in order to achieve your outcome? "If you let me go home at lunchtime today, then I won't ever ask you for time off again."

A **COMPROMISE**. What are you prepared to trade in order to achieve your outcome? "If you let me go home an hour earlier, then I will make it up tomorrow."

The key to all of the above is to have worked out what you're prepared to give way on before the negotiation begins.

The N-word

Now we come to one of the most overlooked skills you can apply in your quest for perfect balance. It is also a wonderful way to illustrate the difference between the hard way to rebalance parts of your life and the Calm Way.

By now you have a clear idea of how perfect balance could work for you. You've explored, and perhaps even taken, many of the steps required to reach this goal. But, frequently, one thing stands in your way.

It's acknowledging your limits. This is more than knowing when to stop, because deep down you already know that. It's knowing *how* to stop.

You are acutely aware that your work and social pressures increase as you take on more responsibilities. Yet if you're like most of us, you'll feel increasingly pressed to accept them—not because you want to or think it's a good idea but because you find it difficult to say no.

When an acquaintance invites you to dinner on a night you'd rather spend at home with a book, you don't like to turn them down. Or when a local charity asks you to sit on a fundraising committee, you feel obliged to agree.

This kind of compliance can be even more pronounced in the workplace. When a colleague asks you to help out with a project, your inclination is to help. When your boss asks you to take on a new responsibility, you want to agree to it.

We have been conditioned to see the virtue in saying yes, even if it means we suffer as a result. It starts in childhood: we want to be seen as cooperative and obedient to authority figures such as parents and teachers. In adolescence, we do it to please our friends and acquaintances. Then, when we finally arrive in the workplace, we become even more agreeable because we believe that advancement is more likely to come from saying yes than no. (Interestingly, people who enter an organization at senior levels, rather than having to work their way up through the ranks, seem to be more adept at saying no.)

> The Calm Way: You can quickly improve your life balance by learning how to say "no" when appropriate, and doing so in the most positive way.

It's human nature to want to say yes. It makes you feel good about helping someone else. Maybe you feel honored to have been asked. By contrast, you're reluctant to say no because you don't like letting someone down. Or maybe you feel there's a degree of confrontation implicit in refusal.

So your inclination is to take the path of least resistance and say yes, even though your mind might be shouting no.

Yes works for the short term; no, for the long term. Yes brings momentary gratification, which you may pay for in the future; no brings a moment of wretchedness but less strain in the long term.

Often, when you say yes to one thing, you're essentially saying no to something else. This is particularly so in the workplace. So cultivating the ability to say the N-word, when appropriate, can make a substantial improvement to your overall life balance.

Positively no

Throughout this book I've encouraged you to think and act positively. Given the choice, you'd rather respond positively to every request. After all, no one likes to deliver a flat no. It sounds negative. It may offend or hurt feelings. It might be detrimental to your career.

Would you like to learn to say no in a positive and constructive way? Yes? Here's how.

- Rationalize your refusal. There's a difference between a rationale and an excuse. An excuse is "I'm doing something else." A rationale is "If I take on what you're asking, I won't have time to complete the other tasks you wanted finished today." One seeks to be excused; the other explains why you can't comply.

   Rationalizations are most applicable when you're dealing with a partner, an adult family member, or a professional superior.

- Offer an alternative. If someone asks for your assistance and you don't want to provide it, there's a way you can satisfy your inclination to help without impacting too much on your workloads or responsibilities. Just offer an alternative. "I can't work overtime today, but I'm more than happy to do it tomorrow."

   Or: "I can't go on that camping weekend with you, but I can suggest a very nice person who might."

Or: "I don't have time to collect your suits from the dry cleaner, but I can bring home a nice bottle of Chardonnay."

So, even though you might not have complied as they'd hoped, you've at least taken some of the sting out of saying no.

- Quickly offer short-term help. This is perhaps the easiest way to satisfy your desire to say yes, without taking on any long-term responsibilities or commitment. It's to do with short-term assistance and a partial fulfillment of the request. We call it the "I can't . . . but I can" approach.

  "I can't join your new committee, but I can give you all my notes from the previous one."

  "I can't help you paint your apartment, but I can help you do the preparation work for the benches."

  As long as you are disciplined about this, and don't let it become an opportunity for further requests, the "I can't . . . but I can" approach can be very useful.

If you want to have a positive influence on the overall balance of your life, learn to use the N-word. If you have a full life and schedule, this could be one of the most important understandings you take from this book. Just remember that you now have a choice in how you respond to a request. Yes, if it will help you achieve what you want (compare it to your Balance Vision). Yes, if it helps somebody in need, without seriously impacting on your own needs. And use the N-word for all other requests.

The final adjustment

If you've followed the advice in the preceding pages, all that stands between you and perfect balance is patience. Perhaps you still have some work to do. Perhaps it's within easy reach. Perhaps you're there already. Whatever stage you're at, you now have the resources to complete the journey.

You know exactly where you want to end up: it's there on your Balance Vision, a visual or verbal summary of what gives your life meaning and motivation, and a balancing point for all your different roles, needs, and pressures.

You've examined the many different roles you play or are expected to play and have prioritized them to some degree. You may also have explored how the balance between them can be fine-tuned or adjusted to achieve the holistic ideal you have in mind.

You produced a strategy for each of these adjustments. And evaluated ways that could help you do it: practical changes, attitudinal changes, scheduling, and dealing with other people's needs and expectations. Now it is time to put all of what's gone before into play.

No more theories. No more postponements or cogitation. Now's the time for action, for moving ahead. It's the time to start enjoying each of the steps for what they are rather than what they will achieve. Throw yourself into them. Enjoy them. Once you start doing this, perfect balance starts to take shape of its own accord.

Whether or not you are conscious of it yet, it has already begun. If you've followed the steps up to now, it will be happening.

How noticeable this will be varies from person to person. Sometimes the changes will be obvious and immediate. More often they will be subtle and cumulative. As with an exercise program, the benefits tend to sneak up on you. You immerse yourself in the routine, focusing on the process rather than the outcome, enjoying it for what it is, without being particularly aware of any changes. Then one day somebody says, "Hey, you look fantastic!" and you start to see yourself in a new light.

Perfect balance arrives like that.

One final note: the adjustments you are making or have made are ongoing. A tweak here and there as time moves on is not only acceptable but desirable. But as long as you know where you're headed, and enjoy making the adjustments for their own sake, you will have perfect balance firmly within your grasp.

The Calm Way: Even if it takes a number of steps to find perfect balance, the most rewarding one is the first. Take it now and you'll be one step closer.

9.

The first or
the final step

As you have now discovered, perfect balance is more a state of mind than a state of circumstances.

Sometimes in order to achieve this state of mind, you may need to change the circumstances of your life. Mostly, though, all you need to do is adopt a few physical or psychological methods to help you see your immediate world in a new light. While we have tended to treat the steps in a fairly linear and logical way, it is possible to achieve the same results in a completely intuitive fashion; many do this after producing a powerful Balance Vision for themselves.

Whichever route you took to get here, you should be on the verge of adopting that state of mind now. Where you *feel* your life is in perfect balance. Where, even if you don't have hard and fast evidence, you *sense* that your life is in perfect balance.

Your whole life.

So, in the assumption that you are at or nearing that place now, I'd like to make a bold suggestion. . . .

What if it's perfect now?

Imagine that your life was *almost* perfectly balanced now, and you didn't realize it!

For the past three, four, perhaps more, decades, you've been assailed with the proposition that it's easy to better yourself. You can be richer and happier. You can be slimmer, more muscular, with firmer breasts and the complexion of a twelve-year-old. You can have a better-paying job. You can have a more sensitive and understanding partner. Or employees. Or children. You can have more love, success, fame, and sexual satisfaction than you have now. Dramatically more. Have it now. Have it all! All you have to do is . . .

Underpinning these propositions is a disquieting and not-so-subtle suggestion that you *should* be adopting them in order to better yourself. But should you?

When I began researching this book, I recalled the job my father had when I was a kid. For as long as I can remember, he had to work fifty- to sixty-hour weeks. His work conditions were rough and uncomfortable. Scarcity of work meant he often had to travel long distances. His intention was to buy a business one day. He had no spare time for introspection, goal-setting sessions, or personal-development courses. Yet he loved what he did and believed he was living a well-balanced life.

Many years later I met a carefree old woman who used to work in the laundry of a city hospital. Even though she was well into her seventies, she trudged—an hour each way—to her backbreaking job in the sweltering basement. Her intention was to pay her own way through life and not have to rely on an old-age pension. She, too, thought she was living a fairly well balanced life.

Recently I employed a wonderful stonemason. He also worked as an office cleaner five nights a week. He'd been working this way for more than ten years. His intention was to repay debts from a business that failed some years ago. He loved his family and had a rich, fulfilling relationship with them, but he couldn't remember the last time he was home for a family meal on a weekday. Still, he had no doubt that his life was fulfilling and well balanced.

In each of those cases the person's work circumstances were not all that dissimilar to some of those you hear complained about today—long hours, tough conditions, poor pay, and extensive travel times. Why didn't these people think that their lives were out of balance? How come they were content and happy with what they were dealt, while others might have been miserable?

That question often puzzled me. How could the same set of circumstances create hardship and resentment in one life yet be fulfilling and enjoyable in another? Sure, I could see that it was primarily a state of mind, but what brought it about?

Putting aside the predictable slights about standards and about the difference between achievers and nonachievers, we are left with only one answer: expectation.

On one hand you have someone who accepts what he's been dealt with gratitude and pleasure, and on the other you have someone who expects more. One person gets on with it and enjoys his lot; the other resents the predicament he is "forced" into. One person is fulfilled and happy; the other is restless and discontent.

My purpose in raising this is to illustrate that the difference between contentment and discontent may not be the job, the conditions, the boss, the opportunities, the attitude of others, or even the state of mind. Perhaps—and I emphasize perhaps—the difference is simply expectation.

Expectation means you have an emotional attachment to an outcome. You believe that if one set of circumstances exists, or if you act in a certain way, then a specific result will eventuate. Expectation is always accompanied by a conscious or subconscious effort to exert control. Then, if what you expect fails to eventuate, you feel frustrated; if it does this repeatedly, you become resentful. When expectation applies to events, it leads to disappointment. When it applies to other people's attitudes or behavior, it leads to hurt and misunderstandings. When it applies to yourself, it blinds you to new ways of seeing things.

Only after you have put all expectations aside do you discover that you have the freedom to relax and enjoy life as it unfolds.

Putting expectations aside does not mean abandoning dreams and ambitions. If you *know* what your goal looks like (such as your Balance Vision), it's easier to attain. If you sincerely *want* it to eventuate, there's a strong likelihood it will do so. If your *intention* or your motivation is to make it happen, the likelihood increases dramatically. But if you *expect* it to happen, you'll be disappointed in one way or another.

Goals show you what the result looks like. Intention focuses you on the process that takes you toward a result. Expectation blinds you to everything but the result.

> The Calm Way: Remove your expectations and you'll never be disappointed. You may be pleasantly surprised by what you discover.

Beyond compare

From the very earliest age, society has been building your expectations. Be it the economy, your income, your education, your leisure time, health resources, or the quality of government services, you expect it to continue or to grow. If it fails to meet your expectations, you are disappointed.

Sometimes, though, it can meet your expectations and you'll still be disappointed! Usually this happens when comparison comes into the equation, because comparison, like expectation, goes hand in hand with discontent.

If you think you're well off and then start hearing about colleagues who earn more, achieve more, and work fewer hours than you do, you may start to question the value of what you have. If you think you've got it together and then start meeting people whose jobs allow them more time for their families or their interests, you may be tempted to resent the number of hours you have to put in. If you're happy with what you have but are constantly offered newer, better, bigger, cheaper, smarter, shapelier, more fascinating alternatives to what you have now, you may find yourself contrasting the value of your possessions or relationships with those of others.

Even if you can avoid making comparisons yourself, they're going to be made for you. In this new world of benchmarks and best practice, your performance will be compared with that of others. As will your costs, your productivity standards, and maybe even your attitudes.

Perfect balance will exist when you value and accept exactly what you are and what you have—without expectations of any kind. And without comparison. This is achievable now.

You are able to do this because you already have every resource you need in order to feel happy, content, and whole. If you choose, you are able to feel this way no matter what your workloads, responsibilities, or demands on your time.

It all comes down to two verbs—accept and allow. Accept what is, and allow yourself to appreciate it for what it is.

This should not be confused with inertia. You can decide to

accept and feel satisfied with where you are and what you are experiencing at this very moment, *even if your intention is to change in the days ahead.*

Look back over your list of what's great about your life. If you've been keeping this record, you'll have noted many of the positives in your life, as well as the values and virtues you hold important.

You can make this list even sweeter by adding another of your qualities—uniqueness. You may sometimes overlook this, but you have an essential and irreplaceable role to play in the history and function of the universe. Not just in your immediate world but in the entire universe. From both physical and metaphysical perspectives. Maybe it's only in the most infinitesimal way, but the world would not be the same without you.

Once you *accept* your unique and special place in the world and *allow* yourself to be satisfied and comfortable with it as it is happening, you suddenly discover that everything you need for a perfectly balanced life is right here in front of you.

It's not any one thing. It's a combination of many—the people you love and who love you, the work you do, the abilities you were born with, the skills you've developed, and the luck you've been dealt. This all adds up to making you the unique person you are.

Accept it.

The Calm Way: You're at your most powerful when you're content to be what you are.

Accept and move on

Accepting what is does not prevent you from making changes. There will be many times when you will want something different from what you already have. Something more satisfying, or perhaps more in tune with your Balance Vision.

You may think this is one of those desperate all-or-nothing choices: either get a new job (or partner, etc.) or get on with it. But there is a third way, an in-between option. Instead of changing jobs when dissatisfaction arises, you find ways of adding satisfaction. Instead of changing partners when you feel the shine is wearing off, you find ways of adding more shine. If ever there was a way we could call the Calm Way to overcome dissatisfaction, it would be this.

> The Calm Way: Instead of trying to change the circumstances that cause you dissatisfaction, you change the way you look at them.

I must emphasize that it is not my wish to be prescriptive here. If your decision is to change your circumstances, then make the decision now and go for it. (Use "The big decision" method on page 250 to help you work through this.)

But if your decision is to change the way you look at your circumstances, there are two deceptively simple yet very powerful ways to do this. The first is "A change of perspective" (page 248). The second relates to where you look.

At this very moment, there are billions of things going on around you and within you. Almost all of them take place without your ever noticing. At best, you can focus on a few of these—perhaps only one at any given time. But what you choose to focus on determines your "reality" at that moment.

If you look for what's good and decent, you'll be amazed at how many good and decent things are taking place around you. If you go looking for beauty, you'll find it everywhere, even in places that other people find unpleasant or unsightly. If you go looking for what's stimulating and satisfying about your job, or what's good and interesting about your partner, or what's gratifying about your health or your financial situation, you'll start finding positive things that begin to shape your reality.

Call it illusion if you will, but it's an illusion that will bring you closer to perfect balance. And if you want to get closer faster, consider the time frame.

Perfect balance now

Human beings are the only creatures that have the ability to discriminate about the future and the past. Many of us exercise this ability more than nature intended. Focus too much on the future or the past and you'll start to compare: "Is this as good as it was five years ago?" "Will I be happier in six months' time?" This limits your ability to be happy and content now. Happiness and contentment are activities of the present; they are here to be enjoyed now. And they can *only* be enjoyed now. At this very moment.

"This very moment" exists only as it is happening. It is not a single second in duration, not even a millisecond, because it has no time dimension. So not only is it impossible to measure, it is impossible to analyze or compare with any other event in your life—you can only do that once this moment has passed.

This moment cannot be thought about or dissected; it can only be experienced. Right now, if you let go of what's gone by and what's ahead, you suddenly find yourself in a moment of pure experience. There is nothing mystical about this, you do it often—such as when you really love a pastime or activity and you get so carried away with it that you lose all track of time or place. You used to do this as a matter of course. As a child you were intrigued and fully occupied by a doll, a matchbox, a piece of junk. You didn't think about the future or the past then, or about what you had to do tomorrow or what you learned this morning. You were focused and absorbed by what was happening in the present.

Because this is a holistic experience—as opposed to just a cognitive one—it instantly makes you feel grounded and centered. You feel calm, capable, and secure. Anxiety and regrets vanish. Your capacity to feel, enjoy, and experience is increased. And, best of all, you didn't have to do a single thing to make it happen.

You can be like that now.

When you dedicate yourself wholly to what is before you, allowing yourself to merge with the process so that you do it to the very best of your ability—without judgment or comparison—you create a focused, harmonious state similar to meditation. This is what perfect balance feels like. Without giving it another thought, you can choose to enjoy this state as you read on.

You may choose to use some or all of the methods and techniques in this book to gradually discover the joy of perfect balance. Or you may choose to have perfect balance now. You may choose to make ongoing changes to parts of your life. Or you may choose to *accept* your whole life for what is, and *allow* yourself to make the most of it now. Whatever path you choose, you are making the right choice.

The reason you do this so confidently is because the state of perfect balance is familiar to you. You have been here before. Right now you may be subtly aware of it. Your attention is centered, with no need for thoughts or descriptions. You feel content and secure.

If you choose to be calm now, you are calm. If you choose to be happy and carefree now, you are happy and carefree. If you choose to enjoy a beautiful moment of wellness now, you are enjoying wellness.

Make these choices now, and you will start to feel complete. Everything comes together and makes sense. You are more powerful than you have felt in ages. You are more certain. You are enjoying peace and contentment.

Because you are experiencing perfect balance.

Now.

> The Calm Way: There's no waiting.
> Perfect balance is where you are now.

Your tools

Life balance chart

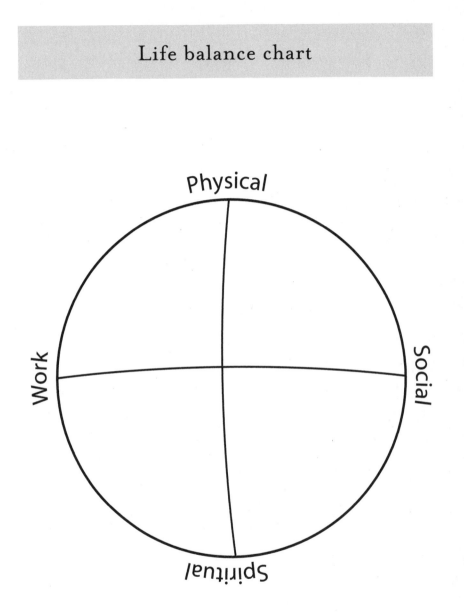

The Calm Way to feel centered

If you've done any yoga, you'll be aware of how a simple change of posture can change the way you feel.

The Calm Way to feel centered is based on this knowledge. It takes place mostly in your imagination, and it is deceptively easy. And while it's subtle, it will quickly have you feeling centered and "in the moment"—if you allow it to. Do this either sitting or standing.

The key to this experiment is a fine strand of string or wire.

- First, slow down your breathing a touch and allow yourself to relax.
- If you're standing, try to imagine your feet being rooted deep into the ground. If you're seated, feel your feet glued to the floor.

- Next, imagine a strand of string or wire attached to an imaginary hook on the top of your head. Pass this imaginary thread through an imaginary pulley on the ceiling above you.
- Imagine that someone is tugging gently on the end of the wire. As it tightens, little by little, your vertebrae start to straighten.
- Bit by bit, allow yourself to feel your entire body starting to lighten.
- Continue this until you feel you are hovering a whisker above the chair or the floor, and your body feels light and relaxed.
- Consider that feeling for a moment. That *centered* feeling. Now, relax and enjoy it.

That simple, physiological change is all it takes for most people to withdraw their attention from the distraction of the outside world, and to get a brief sensation of what it feels like to be centered and in the moment.

Time line

The time-line exercise is designed to help you shift your attention away from the past and the future and to fix it firmly in the present. In this way, instead of the present moment being something that's just squeezed between what's happened and what's about to happen, it fills your consciousness.

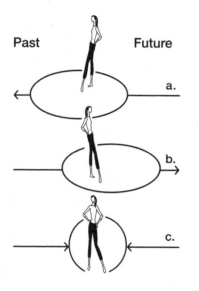

a.   Close your eyes and visualize time stretching back into the past. "Look" behind you. It doesn't matter what you can see, as long as you have an impression of where the past lies.

b.   Next, take your imagination into the future. "Look" ahead of you. Form an impression of where the future lies.

c.   Now, gradually bring the images of past and future toward you until you can feel it here now.

When you visualize that these two impressions have come together, your attention will be wholly in the present.

The big-picture solution

This step involves using your brain in a way that many people routinely avoid throughout their workday. In fact, this is the opposite of the "businesslike thinking" style we referred to earlier.

As you know, your brain has two hemispheres (left and right), each with its own individual processing style.

Essentially, the left is detail-oriented. It's the verbal or word-oriented side. It is associated with structured, linear, analytical thought processes. This is why you favor the left hemisphere during your workday. The left is also associated with life's more stressful activities such as work, structured thinking, and concentration on detail.

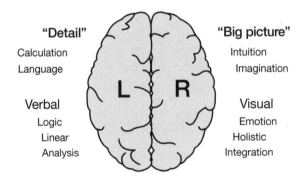

In contrast, the right hemisphere of your brain is holistic in its orientation—imaginative, intuitive, emotive. It's the visual side. The fun and playful side. When you use your mind this way, you find it easier to see the big picture. The right is also associated with life's more relaxing activities.

To take advantage of your right brain's big-picture perspective, you simply adopt a more visual or emotive working style. You need a BIG drawing pad and some colored pencils or pens.

- Your starting point is deciding where you want to end up. "At the completion of this exercise, I will have solved . . ."

- Now, relax for a few minutes and center your attention. (Use "The Calm Way to feel centered" from page 238 or "Time line" from page 240.)

- Instead of using concentrated brainpower to analyze and make decisions—as you'd do in the workplace—use your drawing pad and pens and have a bit of fun. Make big notes (no sentences) or sketches. Try doodling for a change. Remember, this is a mental exercise, not an artistic one.

- Instead of using words or brainpower to work through each issue, just scribble down what *feels* right. Yes, what feels right. Here there's more to be gained from what you sense or feel is right than from what you think. If a picture comes to mind, make a quick note of it. If they're words or ideas, do likewise. Place more emphasis on your intuition or imagination than on your logical or analytical abilities. If you can "see" what something looks like in your imagination, put your faith in what *looks* right rather than what logic tells you must be right.

- After half an hour or so of this, take a short break. Now it's time to think through your notes and doodles and put them into some sort of logical, meaningful shape for yourself. Take your time, try to make sense of it, and trust your instincts.

The moment is now

Never before in history have we been so conscious of time and productivity—the notion of achieving more with the same resources (time and money) or achieving the same with fewer resources. Either way, you end up feeling overworked, with not enough hours in the day.

While the following will do nothing toward reducing the amount of work you believe you have to do, it will work wonders in helping you feel more comfortable about what you're doing, and the time in which you have to do it.

It all boils down to a little Zen philosophy.

There is just one moment in life when workloads and deadlines don't exist, when you believe you have all the time in the world, when there are no regrets about the past or concerns about the future: that moment is right now.

Time does not exist in its own right; it's just an ongoing succession of "nows" for each and every one of us.

This moment you are experiencing is not something you can think about or analyze as it is happening—you can only do that in retrospect. Stressful thoughts or feelings of dissatisfaction cannot exist when you are fully immersed in the present, in this one particular moment of now.

- The key to this is to do only one thing at a time and to do it as thoroughly as you possibly can.

  Whether you're writing a document, entering data, or doing the dishes, commit to the task as conscientiously and skillfully as you can.

  Commit to the process.

- Try to exclude all external stimuli such as a radio or conversation.
- Concentrate on each step of your activity. Give it your full attention. Be aware of the fluid nature of what you're doing; find satisfaction in the process and the detail.
- Soon you will be totally absorbed by what you are doing, and the task will just "do itself." Then you will be calm, relaxed, and centered.

Putting worries in their place

Worry and anxiety have a lot in common. Both are imagination-based, both are future-based, and both usually lack substance.

The nature of worry is to be concerned about something that *might* happen. It is never about something that is taking place at this particular moment—although you will usually believe your problem is both real and present.

Irrational worries can be lessened in intensity, if not eradicated altogether, by taking the following rational steps.

1. Plan for the long term as well as the short term because knowing what to expect helps to alleviate worry.
2. Put your plan in writing.

The next step removes worry from the mental realm altogether, and moves it into the practical.

- This uses a similar method to "The big decision" on page 250. Take a pen and a piece of paper and write your worry at the bottom of the page. At the top of the page write what you'll have achieved when the worry no longer exists.
- On the left, list all impediments that stand in your way to achieving this. On the right, list all the possibilities or the resources you have to help you achieve it.

In most cases, the worry you recorded at the bottom of your page will seem less threatening or will vanish altogether by the time you've completed the exercise.

A stretch of the imagination

Despite what you were taught in the classroom, rational thought processes can be the single greatest obstacle to changing the way you think.

If you want to adopt a new attitude or way of looking at things, you need to be able to step away from your everyday structured, linear thinking and tap into your intuition, emotion, and the wealth of unconscious resources you hardly ever use. The way to do this is through your imagination.

The saying "a picture is worth a thousand words" was never more appropriate than when used to describe a mental picture's influence on your subconscious. If you feed your subconscious with powerful visual images, it puts logic and judgment aside and takes those images onboard in a totally uncritical way. This is why visualization is such a favored tool in psychotherapy.

Strangely, many people find the concept of visualization to be a bit alien. "I've never been able to visualize" is the protest we most often hear. Yet in almost all cases this apparent limitation is overcome with a simple change of terminology. So, instead of going on about visualization, from now on we will refer to a skill that you mastered at a tender age—imagining. Or fantasizing.

There are three keys to doing this successfully.

1. Always choose *positive* things to imagine. For example, imagine yourself as a smiling, successful employee—not as someone who has overcome the frustrations of a difficult boss.
2. Choose an imagined result that best sums up the way you'd like to *feel*. If you're feeling overworked and highly stressed, imagine yourself feeling calm, relaxed, and completely in control at work.

3. Get all your senses working at once. Imagine what you'll hear when you are this relaxed, successful employee. Imagine any physical changes—textures, temperatures, fragrances.

These are the steps to follow.

- Put aside half an hour for the exercise. Choose a quiet place where you won't be disturbed. Take a large pad and pencil.
- Allow yourself to relax, letting go of all thoughts, reassuring yourself that you have all the time in the world should you need it.
- As you feel yourself start to relax, let your imagination drift to this idea of how you'd like to be. For 20 minutes or so, just let go and imagine you are this person.
- Now that you can imagine what it's like to be this person, you might also be able to imagine what you're feeling, hearing, and seeing.
- Because this enriches the experience for you, you might be able to imagine—not in detail but in a very subtle, perhaps subconscious way—what it would take for you to remain like this at all times. How good would that feel?
- Enjoy the feeling. Let it remain with you. What does it take for you to feel this way? If anything comes to mind—whether it makes sense or not—jot it down. If you feel like drawing, let the broad picture come. If you feel like writing, write in large letters only.

When you've exhausted your top-of-mind thoughts and ideas, you can evaluate what's on your pad—if anything. You can be as linear as you like because this is the interpretation phase. Work out what steps need to be taken (if any), and formalize any plans that may be required.

A change of perspective

You immediately begin to feel you have some control over a situation when you recognize that it presents you with a choice: you either change the situation that bothers you or you change the way you look at it.

Changing the situation can be difficult; you can't fire the board, or alter government regulations, or change your partner's personality. But, in all cases, you can change the way you view the situation. This is not difficult to accomplish if you follow a few simple steps.

Do this somewhere quiet, where you will not be interrupted for half an hour.

- First, be aware of what's important and what takes priority in your life.

- Next, be aware of how you'd like to be once you've changed your perspective. This takes place in your imagination, so have fun with it. What will you look or sound like if you are no longer afraid of your boss? Or if you can easily cope with all the demands being made on your time? Or if you really loved the job you have? Or if you feel skillful and in control of the tasks you have to perform? Choose positive mental pictures that you can project onto your subconscious.

- When you can imagine what that scenario looks like, imagine yourself as part of it. What do you look like? What are the details of the setting?

- Now, instead of just "seeing" this scenario in your imagination, imagine what it's like to be part of it. What are you seeing? What are you hearing? What are you feeling and sensing? The more detail you provide here, the more influence it has on your subconscious.

- When you are immersed in this imaginary experience, take a mental snapshot of the scene, complete with all the images, sounds, and feelings.

Keep this mental snapshot foremost in mind as you revisit the original situation (in your imagination). Repeat the exercise until what you feel is to your liking.

The big decision

Often, the most important decisions of your life are made with a sense of trepidation and with no clear strategy in mind. The trepidation is understandable, since big decisions can change the direction of your life and can also involve a degree of risk.

The secret to inspired decision making is quite straightforward: just put your analytical abilities on hold for a while and complete the following steps.

- To start with, explore as many different possible choices as you can think up. Make sure to include a few wild ideas here as well as sensible ones.
- In your notebook, make a list of 10 of these ideas. Yes, 10.
- Now, totally ignoring what you "know" to be workable or appropriate, tick off those you *feel* you'd like to explore. This is the list you're going to be working with.

	+	**−**
1		
2		
3		
4		
5		
6		
7		
8		
9		
10		

- Review your shortened list and, once again, disregard any you *feel* are inappropriate. You should have 2–4 options remaining.
- Now turn to a new page of your notebook.
- With a "+" column on the left and a "–" on the right, make a list of the advantages and disadvantages of each option.
- As you do this, allow your intuition and feelings to have full rein. If one approach *feels* right, but logic tells you to discard it, keep it in.
- Now, weighing up both sides of the argument, what do you *feel* is the right decision?

There are two more steps you need to take to bring this pending decision into the cold hard world of rationality (the head).

- Discuss it with another person. Talking aloud about it is a great way of testing how sensible and "clear-headed" it sounds.
- Once you are committed, announce your decision to at least one person you admire or respect. This turns a mental decision into something that has to be acted on.

Go forward, step back

Some rational thinkers are uncomfortable relying on the popular tools of the subconscious—visualization, imagination, repetition, and suggestion. Usually, they find them to be a bit too unempirical for their liking. "It's not scientific." "If I can't see it, hear it, or measure it, I really can't accept that it works."

Frequently, these same people will acknowledge that the structured thinking styles they favor cannot produce the answers they require—but their commitment remains.

Accepting that all people are different and all styles of thinking must ultimately be accommodated if we are to produce results, we developed a way of side-stepping these barriers. This method activates the imagination in a linear, methodical way by employing a common tool that all of us use for planning: thinking about the future.

By its very nature, thinking about the future is an exercise in the abstract. After all, the future does not exist—other than in your imagination. Once you start thinking about the future, your thinking style becomes more right-brain (visual, imaginative). If you relax while you do this, your thinking style changes even more. The more relaxed you are, the more your deeper, hidden resources come to the surface. Now you're more in touch with your emotions and intuition. Rational obstacles start to fade, and subtle insights make themselves known. This is the most powerful way to tap into your innermost thoughts and feelings.

Set aside half an hour for this exercise. Choose a quiet place where you won't be disturbed. Take a large pad and a thick pen or pencil. Then work through the following steps.

- **GO FORWARD.** In your imagination, go forward to a time in the future. You have achieved whatever result you aimed for. What are you like now? Try to describe your appearance. What is the look on your face? How are you standing or sitting? What are you wearing? Try to describe your surroundings. Are there any sounds? Any textures? Breeze, temperature, scents, vibrations?

- Mentally, try to describe what you're feeling. Is it a strong, intelligent frame of mind? Are you in complete control? Do you have an idea of what others might be thinking?
- **STEP BACK**. Now, let's come back a few days (or months) from that future occasion. When you can sense this place in time, mentally ask yourself, "What steps did I take to get here?" You may not get a clear-cut answer, but you'll definitely *have an idea*.
- Now that you're getting the hang of this, you can come back even further—halfway between "then" and "now." When you have a firm grasp of this place in time, ask yourself, "What steps did I take to get here?" Once again, though you might not be able to put this into words, you'll definitely *have an idea* of what it took.
- Now, you can come back to this very moment. Off the top of your head, without thinking or trying to imagine anything, sketch, note, or write down five things you did to achieve the result you were thinking about at the beginning of this exercise.
- Once you have five "hints" on the pad, you can get to work interpreting them, fleshing them out, and making them more practical.

When using this technique, you have all your subconscious resources helping you to find answers that you can consciously interpret.

Time to rebalance

Every human being needs space and quiet moments in the day to restore and maintain equilibrium.

Rather than tell yourself there's no spare time in your day for this, reward yourself with 20–30 minutes of "therapy" time, where you allow your thoughts and physiology to rebalance. If you can find an hour, even better. If you must, schedule in a meeting with yourself.

"Time to rebalance" requires no structure, effort, or training. In fact, it has no inherent purpose other than to let you *be*. To be yourself. Be relaxed. Be calm. Be restored.

- Remember, there is no agenda.
- Go somewhere peaceful and quiet. Take yourself for an extended stroll. Sit in the park or the garden. Take time on a long bus ride. Lock yourself in the bathroom and put out your real or imaginary "DO NOT DISTURB" sign. I'm sure you'll think of some way of allowing yourself the space you need.

- Listen to the sound of your relaxed breathing as you allow yourself to ease back into a calm, restful state. Tell yourself you have all the time in the world.
- When your thoughts drift outward—to your duties and responsibilities in the outside world—slowly bring them back to yourself, to the relaxed state you are in. (Try to occupy yourself with what you're feeling rather than what you're thinking.)

And that's really the extent of the exercise.

If you approach this without expectation and with an open mind, you'll discover that this simple exercise can become a pleasure you'll look forward to as time goes on. It's not entertainment or a stimulation; nor is it an obligation or a regime you have to adhere to. It's just a simple, guilt-free pause that will help you appreciate how important *you* are to finding a life of perfect balance.

You can take this experience into other parts of your life. Schedule a few minutes at work, on the bus, between engagements, or before lunch to add a stress-free buffer to your day.

Once you make a practice of this, you'll become addicted to these moments. You'll think nothing of using some of your shower time, or foregoing half an hour of television or reading time in an evening, or even rising a little earlier to indulge in it. Because it will mean that the remainder of your day will be enhanced and enriched.

Deep Calm

Deep Calm is a variation on a number of traditional meditation and yoga practices. It is a big topic in itself, and it has been the subject of a number of my books. Here is a simplified version of it.

The relaxed state that it produces will be familiar to you. It's not unlike the feelings you associate with daydreaming, or the moments before dozing off, or when you lose track of time on a long train or bus ride. On those occasions you weren't aware of anything out of the ordinary taking place, or of any particular state of mind, you were just . . . being. This is what Deep Calm feels like and how it works.

Deep Calm comes about without any directed effort on your part. In fact, the more effort you apply, the less successful you will be. The object is to relax, without expectation, and let it happen.

Unlike most things that go on in your consciousness, Deep Calm happens—quite naturally—when you stop thinking. It's as simple as that. The problem is that most people can't just still their thoughts on command. No amount of willpower will do it. The only way to consciously manage it is to occupy your mind with something else— an image, a fantasy, a feeling, a sound, a repetitive action, a word, or a phrase—leaving no room for thinking. Then Deep Calm happens of its own accord.

- First, find yourself a place where you can sit and relax without interruption for 10–20 minutes.
- Take the phone off the hook.
- Use "The Calm Way to feel centered" from page 238. This will help withdraw your attention from the outside world so that you feel centered and balanced.

- As you begin to relax—and you are beginning to relax when you do this—your breathing starts to slow just a little until it is unhurried and relaxed.
- Now, all you have to do is listen to the sound of your breath as you breathe out. You will probably be able to hear it clearly as you breathe in, but concentrate on that sound as you breathe out. Just listen. Listen to the sound of your breath as you breathe out.
- There is nothing else you have to do. Just listen to that sound, and you begin to slow down. And as you *listen*, with each breath you exhale, you become even more relaxed. You slow down even more.

There are only two barriers you may encounter.

The first one occurs only in the early days of experimenting with Deep Calm. After a few minutes of going through the exercise, you begin to wonder whether there's anything further you should be doing. How can something so simple possibly work? Surely there must be more to it than this. But there's not. Repetition is the key. And after you've persisted for a while, the most pleasant, calm state will overtake you. This is the way your physiology works.

The second barrier is a perennial one, but it is easily dealt with. It relates to thoughts. Considering that the purpose of Deep Calm is to still your thoughts, any occurrences of them might seem like the most unwelcome of intrusions. Yet they are an integral part of the process. If thoughts come—which they will—consider them a passing occurrence to be treated with indifference. They'll be there for a few seconds or minutes before you realize, "Hey, I'm thinking again." When this happens, gently return your attention to the sound of your breathing. As you become more experienced, one of the insights you will discover is that moving on from uninvited thoughts actually moves you closer to the state of Deep Calm.

Please remember, though, that Deep Calm is meant to be as simple as it appears. It is not a test of concentration or willpower. And the experience doesn't have to be anything special in itself.

In many ways it's like an exercise program—the benefits seem subtle at first, but they keep on growing. If you find your initial enthusiasm beginning to wane after a month or so, focus even more because this is precisely the time that you start to notice the next level of benefits beginning to emerge.

If you're interested in taking this further, refer to www.thecalmway.com/meditation

Setting goals

Well-defined goals are a prerequisite to success. They help you identify what's important so you don't waste time and energy on the unimportant stuff.

In the conventional sense, goal setting is a fairly formal planning process in which you determine exactly what you want to achieve, complete with the various targets or benchmarks that will help you achieve this.

Unlike strategic thinking, which is usually a rational process, goal setting can be more emotional in nature. Because goals are future-related, they are usually an aspect of imagination.

Most people think the most important part of goal setting is establishing accurate and measurable targets. But there's much more to it than this. A well-defined goal should be framed in such a way that it not only sums up what you intend to accomplish but actually begins to program your mind and emotions into starting the journey.

You take a big step toward achieving this through the words you use. Include the following attributes and your goal will become much more compelling.

- PERSONAL. Personal words like "I," "we," "us," and "our" are essential. You can't create goals for other people.
- POSITIVE. Every goal has to be about doing something, rather than *not* doing it. "Learning not to be angry" is nowhere near as powerful as "Learning to be even-tempered and accepting of other opinions."
- TANGIBLE. Describe how you will measure it. The more specific the time frames and parameters, the more likely they are to be reached.

- SENSORY. Use sensory-based terms. What will it *look* like when I've accomplished this? What will I hear? How will I feel?

Pay particular attention to this last step. It is an area that is largely ignored, but it will make your goals much more compelling.

Having clear goals gives your life direction. They give you a sense of autonomy. They make it easier to keep all aspects of your life in perspective. If a great "opportunity" comes along, you weigh it up in the context of your goals—if it fits, steam ahead and take advantage of it; if it clashes, walk away. Or if a problem arises, evaluate it in accordance with your goals—if it must be overcome to satisfy your goals, give it all your effort and attention; but if it has no bearing on them, save your energy for something more important.

The Life Priorities Calculator

The Calm Way to get your life in order

There are choices and opportunities whichever way you turn.
Can you respond to them quickly? Or do they become just
another pressure you have to cope with?

You may not be aware of them at this moment, but there are choices and opportunities all around you.

If one of them were to thrust itself in front of you now—unexpected but packed with potential—would you be in the position to act on it? Could you accept or reject it with confidence, knowing you'd made a decision you wouldn't regret?

Or would you have to offer some sort of excuse like, "Sorry, but I'm not sure I can afford that right now." Or, "Sorry, but I think my job is progressing okay at the moment." Or, "Sorry, but I think I'll be doing something else at that time."

That's the trouble with opportunities. If you're not certain where you're headed, even the greatest opportunity can be a frustrating distraction.

There are everyday events that some people find overwhelming,
yet others take them in their stride. What does it take
to be able to take things in your stride?

Most of the events that cause us concern throughout the day—the worries, the insecurities, and the inevitable work and social pressures—are the product of perception rather than reality.

It's more a matter of what we think is expected of us, rather than what actually is. Or what might happen, rather than what is likely to happen.

If you have a firm grasp of what's most important in your life, you'll find it easier to keep life's ups and downs in perspective.

> There's an important decision to be made, right now. Can you
> make it with ease and confidence? Or does it become yet
> another responsibility you have to deal with today?

The difference between life and death, or success and failure, can often be the simplest decision.

You have to make decisions every day of your life. Most are mundane, but now and then a big one comes along. Say it's a critical health, relationship, or career issue. Could you make the necessary decision with confidence—in the sure knowledge that you wouldn't regret it later?

Or would you have to postpone? Sweat over it until the moment had passed? Hand over the responsibility to someone else? Take a wild stab of what you think *might* be the best way to go?

That's the problem with big decisions: unless you know exactly how they relate to all other aspects of your life, they can be a burden.

> You need more balance in your life. More time for your
> family and yourself, ideally at the same time as you get ahead.
> Do you know what to concentrate on, and what to let go?
> Or do you struggle to fit it all in?

All you do is work. Not enough time for family or friends. No time to ease off and enjoy things. There has to be more to life than this.

You repeatedly tell yourself these things. You resolve that it's going to be different from now on. You're definitely going to reorder the activities of your life, get your priorities in order.

But how can you get your priorities in order if you've never worked out exactly what your priorities are?

Getting your priorities in order is your first priority

The many priorities in your life

It's probably stating the obvious to say that the purpose of the Life Priorities Calculator is to help you determine your life's priorities.

You might wonder why you need a calculator to highlight the things that may be adding pressure to your life today—after all, you know them well.

Come to think of it, there are probably many more priorities in your life than you'd ever asked for. With very little effort, you could probably list three or four of them right now. The big question is, can you have more than one priority at a time?

By definition, a priority implies a ranking—one thing being more important or urgent than another. The very notion that you can have multiple priorities at the same time goes against the meaning of the word.

This is not just an issue of definition.

The more priorities you believe you have at any given time, the more pressure you will feel. This is how the human mind works.

I emphasize this point in all my books: Dividing your attention creates tension and restlessness, whereas focusing on only one thing is calming and fulfilling. Dividing your attention reduces your effectiveness, whereas focusing on only one thing makes you more efficient. Dividing your attention limits performance; focusing improves it.

You'll have seen this demonstrated in your own life: trying to do many things at once tends to compromise all of them, whereas focusing on only one task—approaching it wholeheartedly, performing it to the best of your abilities—not only produces a better result but is also the most satisfying way to work.

You may think I'm talking about an ideal world here, in which you enjoy the luxury of having only one priority that you have to concentrate on at a time. You're right. That would be an ideal world. However, just because it's ideal doesn't mean it's unattainable. Quite the contrary.

How do you rank them?

If you knew all your priorities, and how—or if—they should be ranked, you wouldn't have read this far.

Isn't it amazing how we can make our way through life—day in day out at the same job; persevering with the ups and downs of moods, finances, and relationships; feeling healthy, ill, enlightened, confused, inspired, depressed—without ever seriously pausing to ask, "What's the purpose of all this? What takes precedence in my life?"

There are times when you ask yourself these questions, of course, but generally these occur only when you reach crossroads in your life:

- when you're finishing high school or college
- when you're evaluating or leaving a relationship
- when you're changing jobs
- when you've been laid off
- when you turn forty (or so)
- when you have a child
- when you become aware of your own mortality through illness or the death of someone close
- when you contemplate retirement
- when you face the end of your days.

Yet most of the action, most of your accomplishments or failures and indeed most of your opportunities for happiness and fulfillment occur in the times between. *These* are the key times of your life.

It would be a tragedy if they passed and you hadn't gotten around to deciding what you really felt was most important to you.

What some people think is important

Several years ago my research group at the Calm Centre conducted a study into workplace attitudes, ostensibly to explore how today's employee handles work pressure. One of our questions was "How do you rank the various drives, influences, ambitions, and responsibilities that make up your life? What's most important?"

Simple questions on the surface, yet we were surprised at just how few people could answer them with any degree of comfort and insight.

In the main, the "priorities" most people mentioned related to either:

- immediate problems—such as health, relationships, child care, or work; or
- financial, career, or lifestyle goals.

How can solving problems and achieving performance benchmarks be considered life priorities? When you're old and wrinkled, and your grandchildren want to know what you did with your time on earth, surely you'll want more to talk about than "I figured out a way to postpone my mortgage payment in July," or "I signed up thirty percent more customers in 2004 than I did in 2003."

Clearly we have to look beyond immediate problems to be solved and assorted goals to be met.

What do you think is important?

When you look beyond the obvious, what do you know about yourself? What makes you tick? Can you articulate your personal values and motivations? Can you easily rank the things most important to you? Can you nominate a purpose in life?

If you balk at these questions, you might take comfort in the fact that most people wrestle with them.

Although we haven't explored what people believe their "purpose in life" is—but we will later, in the "Finding purpose" chapter—I know from Calm Centre interviews that this is a question more people ask than answer.

Let's try a few more questions:

- Does your life move forward with purpose? Or do you plod on one day after another, responding to whatever comes your way?
- Does what you do each day have meaning and value? Or do you just do what you have to in order to get by?

- Do you know what you want to achieve from your daily routine? Or do you want different things at different times of the day, depending on your whims or passing influences?
- Do you have the best occupation and relationship that you can possibly have?
- Are you making the most of your time on this planet?

Once again, if you can't answer these questions, you're in good company. Perhaps your life is too busy to permit such self-examination. Perhaps you haven't really seen the importance before now. Perhaps you're unwilling to face up to answers that may be disagreeable or too revealing. Or perhaps . . . well, there's always tomorrow.

Because it can be an enjoyable exercise in its own right, the Life Priorities Calculator will give you the inspiration you need to overcome these obstacles and really take stock of what's important.

Bringing order to your priorities

I've mentioned the importance of having your priorities "in order." There are a number of reasons why this is important.

Foremost is that it will help you cultivate a sense of inner calm and balance—so you can throw yourself into your busy, demanding life while enjoying a peaceful sense of order and control.

Next on the list is the simple matter of efficiency. Just as you cannot pursue several goals at once or serve several masters at once, you cannot balance several priorities. Yet you'd be surprised at how many people try to do just this. Referring back to that workplace study by the Calm Centre, we discovered that:

- all the people interviewed had multiple priorities in their life;

- most believed that it was not only possible but essential to manage them all simultaneously.

This is a recipe for disappointment. Whether or not it's possible for you to manage multiple priorities at one time, there's a significant price to pay for attempting it—you'll feel restless and under pressure, your efficiency levels will drop, and you won't get anywhere near the satisfaction that's possible from what you do in your work, with your family, or from any other avenue of life.

This is why it's vital to be able to rank the priorities in your life according to their importance to you.

Importance can be calculated

There are all sorts of drives, influences, and responsibilities that shape your immediate world. On top of this, there are many competing areas that you choose or are expected to focus your efforts on. Are all these areas necessary? Are they equally important? Or can some be shed, or postponed, or rearranged while you concentrate on others?

It's widely believed that in this day and age there are no simple answers to questions like these. The argument is that life is more complex today and that merely to survive takes more time and effort than it did in days gone by. And that, despite the obvious strains and limitations, having to deal with multiple priorities is an aspect of modern living we have to accept.

This is a loser's argument.

Like no other period in history, today's world is rich with choices and opportunities. To be able to capitalize on them, all you need are a few skills and abilities. The major one is being able to define what your priorities are, so you can concentrate on what's important to you rather than dissipating your energies over a spread of imagined needs, obligations, and responsibilities.

To be able to do this, you need a framework in which to evaluate the daily pressures and demands that confront you. Determining this framework is not rocket science. But unless you have a pain-saving method such as the Life Priorities Calculator, it can be a formidable task.

Why?

For a start, most people approach it the hard way: they begin with their top-of-mind needs or problems, then try to reason their way forward from there. They quickly discover this takes them nowhere.

Even when they try to adopt a more holistic approach, they discover that this, too, is difficult and unpredictable. Because the majority of human drives and needs are either subconscious or unconscious, we're simply not aware of their presence, even while they're influencing most of what we do and feel.

A far more effective way is the reverse of this—the Calm Way—using the Life Priorities Calculator.

Because it relies on both your conscious *and* subconscious resources, the Life Priorities Calculator is a wonderfully simple way to work out exactly what makes you tick—superficially as well as at the deepest levels.

This allows you to see through the distractions of day-to-day life so you can identify what's important, at whatever stage of life you're experiencing.

So whether you use it once a year, every few months, or even more regularly, the Life Priorities Calculator will help you get your priorities in order. You can then use this knowledge as a foundation to help you:

- get everyday life events into perspective
- make sound decisions
- quickly evaluate opportunities and choices
- adjust the balance between the competing elements of your life
- recognize and set appropriate goals
- scale back or increase your efforts in the activities in which you are presently involved.

A lesson in objectivity

Over the past couple of decades I've worked closely with many corporations, helping them to define or redefine their priorities at various stages of their evolution.

In many instances, what impressed me about this process was the dispassionate way some corporations would go about evaluating themselves—what they were good at, what they wanted to achieve, what stood in their way, and so on. (Not all organizations do this, of course, but the successful, harmonious ones tend to have a fairly clear idea of what they're about.)

If you could be this objective about yourself, imagine how much easier it would be to work out your life's priorities!

While most of the successful, fulfilled people I've met are very aware of their personal values and priorities, it's not easy for most of us to be objective about these things.

For obvious reasons, we tend to be emotionally involved in how we assess ourselves. You may have heard of the theory of self-perception that, in effect, says we're just not very good at working out what drives us or what's behind our attitudes or limitations. We tend to evaluate ourselves in much the same way that an onlooker would: we look at what we're doing and then draw conclusions about the reason we're doing it. For example, "I'm working long hours, therefore I must have an awful lot of responsibilities on my plate." This back-to-front interpretation usually overlooks the real reason.

In addition to this, our lives are made up of programmed responses. Without giving it a second thought, we automatically answer X if someone asks us Y. We automatically think A if someone mentions B. Often there is no sense or logic to these responses—it's just conditioning.

To avoid these pitfalls, the Life Priorities Calculator uses a role-playing technique. When you try it, you'll find that it is quite lighthearted and fun.

The paradox in this technique is that it allows you to discover deeply personal aspects of your life and personality while retaining a level of objectivity you would not normally be capable of.

So far you've discovered:
- It's important to decide what's important.
- You will be calmer, more efficient, and happier when you don't have to juggle "multiple priorities" simultaneously.
- Most people don't know how to rearrange their lives so they can rank their priorities.
- There's a hard way, and a Calm Way, of accomplishing this.

The Calm Way
to calculate
your priorities

Forget the hard way

When it comes to getting priorities in order, the approach most people take is the hard way. They tend to focus on top-of-mind needs and problems . . . or they sweat over trying to weed out the important from the not-so-important . . . or they get far too cerebral . . . or they adopt any old hit-or-miss approach because the whole thing's just too hard.

The hard way is confusing, takes you into areas you don't need to go into, and if you really work hard at it will simply make your head hurt. What's more disappointing is that after all that effort you still won't have the clear insight you're looking for.

Is it any wonder that most people never think about priorities until they're facing a crisis or turning point of some sort?

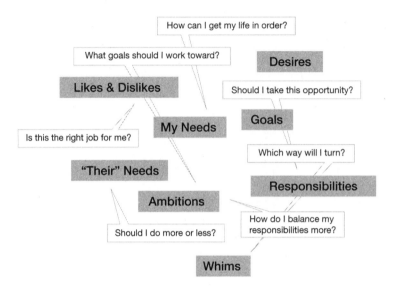

The Calm Way to get your priorities in order

The Life Priorities Calculator is a key part of the Calm Way™ suite of tools. These work on the principle that the best way to accomplish your goals is not by working harder—which can actually be counter-productive—but by taking a more enjoyable and intuitive approach we call the Calm Way. Because it brings all your resources into play at once, the Calm Way results are measurably more effective.

Using the Calm Way principle, the Life Priorities Calculator gives you a streamlined and enjoyable way to bring the priorities in your life into sharp focus. This is an invaluable way to quickly assess what's important and what can wait—so you can make decisions, set goals, take advantage of opportunities, and establish balance in your life.

The CALM Way

How can I get my life in order?

What goals should I work toward?

Which way will I turn?

Is this the right job for me?

Should I take this opportunity?

Should I do more or less?

How do I balance my responsibilities more?

Priorities

The calculator takes you through two very different phases, each using a different part of your brain.

The first phase is the groundwork. It's essential if you're going to be able to use the calculator quickly and easily. This phase is left-brain in nature: logical, straightforward, and involving a bit of detail. It's also more time-consuming than the second—although most of it has to be performed only once.

The second phase is right-brain in nature: intuitive, relaxed, holistic, and streamlined. Better still, it's something you can do as often as you like—for short- as well as long-term purposes.

Once you've completed these two phases, everything will have fallen into place. You will have taken into account all your needs, values, motivations, responsibilities, desires, and ambitions—both conscious and unconscious—in one effortless process.

The Life Priorities Calculator

PHASE I

Easy on four different levels

Before you move on to the Life Priorities Calculator, there are a few decisions to be made. Nothing difficult or work-intensive, just simple, reflective conclusions you'll easily reach about yourself.

To make it even easier, we'll approach these conclusions on four different levels, each of which can be revealing and enjoyable in its own right.

What makes them enjoyable is that they involve nothing much more than just sitting around thinking about your favorite subject—you. Haven't you been waiting for an excuse like this?

Just as you approach these conclusions on four different levels, you should perform them on four separate occasions. (Ideally, on four different days, but you can vary this as you see fit or as your time permits.) Each level can be considered in as much depth as you feel is necessary or desirable. On completion, this adds up to one big picture of all the different influences that shape your life.

The influences in your life

You've probably got by this far in life without being fully aware of how your life's priorities stack up. So getting them into order now is not a matter of leaping in, doing a ten-minute exercise, and then deciding "these are my priorities." Your life is a bit more complex than that.

Priorities do not stand out like eye color or blood type. They are the product of a lifetime of different influences. Some of these influences are obvious, some subtle; some are conscious, some subconscious; some are external, some internal. But they all play a part in your final makeup and motivation.

As I have mentioned, the influences in your life function at four different levels. Even though the order of influence for you may vary, we're going to approach them in this sequence:

- your values
- your needs
- your responsibilities
- your goals, ambitions, or desires.

Each of these categories influences the others. One builds on another.

Your values underpin your needs.

Your needs underpin your responsibilities.

Your responsibilities underpin your goals and ambitions.

To leap from one without taking into account the others, or to start with one without being aware of the one that precedes it, would

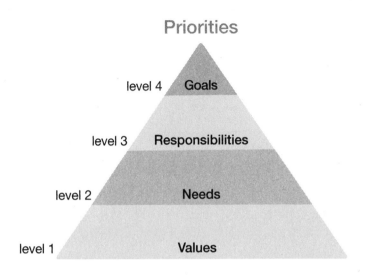

deliver a superficial result. If you want an all-encompassing view of your life's priorities, you first need to have an all-encompassing view of the influences in your life.

To put this into a more visual framework, we're going to build a little pyramid for ourselves—Values at the base (level 1), leading to Needs (level 2), then Responsibilities (level 3), and then Goals (level 4).

Once you have arranged them like this, you'll find it easy to go on and rank your priorities.

LEVEL I: Your values

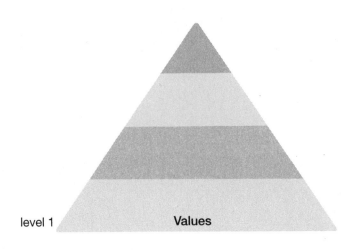

level 1   **Values**

What gives your life meaning?

At the core of most human behavior is a set of values that most of us seldom notice. These are your core values.

Even though you may never think about them, or if you do they may not be immediately apparent, these fundamental qualities or characteristics play a key role in your makeup. In the main, they make you what you are. They give your life direction and meaning. They have a direct influence on everything you feel and think, and much of what you do. They're the reason you sense that one course of action is superior to another. They're how you know something is right or wrong. You use them to justify behavior. They're at the base of life's most satisfying decisions.

True, you can make big decisions based purely on your needs today: you could, for example, choose your life partner because you feel lonely and need someone to be with tonight. Similarly, you can make decisions based solely on today's responsibilities: you could choose your life partner because your children need a parent to replace the one who just walked out. You can also make decisions according to your current goals or ambitions: you could choose your life partner based on their ability to buy you that beautiful new house you've been lusting after.

But the most satisfying, harmonious decisions will be those that are made in accordance with your core values.

Some examples of *positive* human values are truthfulness, responsibility, compassion, and optimism. There are, of course, thousands more.

Given that they play such a large role in shaping your experience of life, it's worth investing the small effort it takes to work out exactly what they are.

Where do they come from?

Your values are closely aligned with your beliefs and attitudes. (Beliefs are things you "know" to be real and put your trust in; attitudes are the way you feel about them. Beliefs stem from your values; attitudes stem from your beliefs.)

Your core values begin to form at a very early age, largely due to the influence of your parents, teachers, and community.

As you grow and are influenced by other people, these values may change or evolve. Usually they will build on the "value foundations" you had from the earliest stages, but this is not always the case. Indeed, there are phases in life where you actually develop conflicts in values—such as when you're a toddler, a teenager, or a young adult. For example, the young adult may experience a conflict between the values of intimacy and isolation—the long-standing need for parental intimacy conflicting with the desire for independence.

Even if your values don't actually change, they do vary in importance at different stages. When you're eighteen years old, you might value life experience more than modesty. But when you reach middle age, life experience probably won't rate so highly, and you may see modesty in a completely different light.

However, as far as your life priorities are concerned, our interest is in your values *right now*.

The meaning of the words

The main hurdle people face when trying to determine their values is one of terminology. People usually interpret the same value in different ways. For example, no two people will extract the same meaning from a value described as "compassion," which probably explains how much conflict arises in relationships and workplaces.

In addition to this, there is often confusion over what is a value, what is a quality, and what is a virtue. Do they relate to one another? Or are they completely different?

For convenience sake, we will put aside the subtle differences in meaning between values, qualities, and virtues and will treat them as one and the same.

And, considering that you're doing this exercise on your own, feel free to interpret each value according to your whim. All that counts is what the word means to you.

Defining your values

Earlier, I mentioned that what I have found instructive about a well-run organization is the dispassionate way it evaluates its qualities—an ability most of us lack as individuals.

Successful organizations not only know what their values are but use them as a foundation for the way they operate. Here are a couple of well-known examples.

- The Red Cross lists its values (or fundamental principles) as: humanity, impartiality, neutrality, independence, voluntary service, unity, and universality. If you worked for or required the services of an organization such as the Red Cross, you'd know exactly what it stood for and what was expected of it.

- Disney has a better-known suite of values: imagination and wholesomeness. If you worked for or patronized an organization with values such as these, you'd know exactly what to expect.

Imagine if you could be that clear-cut about your values. It would give you the perfect foundation to address all the big issues that come your way—without having to sweat over decisions or wonder which direction to head in.

Big organizations can afford to bring in consultants to help them define their values. What are you supposed to do?

Maybe you could choose them from a list.

That would be a start. But some people find choosing the appropriate words to define their values is quite a task. You might *sense* what your values are or you might even *know* them intimately, but you could still struggle to find a word that sums up each one.

I'll give you an example. Here is a list of human values:

- Relationships
- Belonging
- Fun
- Respect
- Accomplishment
- Security

Some people will look at this list and immediately get the picture of what a person holding these values is about. But others will look at it and scratch their heads, because one person's choice of words often won't mean a great deal to another person.

However, if you were to see each of these values expressed in a phrase—before being edited down to a single word—it would be easier to understand:

- Having rich and fulfilling *relationships*.
- Feeling a sense of *belonging*.
- Getting *fun* and enjoyment out of what I do.
- Earning the *respect* of others.
- Feeling that I've accomplished [*accomplishment*] something of worth.
- Feeling a sense of *security* and well-being.

Making this process simple

The two problems we face when trying to highlight human values are: getting a sense of what your values are or what values mean most to you, and then finding words to describe them.

If you try to do it just by sheer brainpower, you'll find it tough going. This is why we're going to use a simple process that not only helps bring your core values to the surface but helps you to describe them in a way that's meaningful to you. Only you.

This process can be an enjoyable experience—providing you don't take it too seriously. There are no right and wrong answers. And the correct way to approach it is any way that feels right for you.

You'll do it in five easy steps. Each one can be a relaxed, almost self-indulgent little look at yourself.

So take your time, don't give another thought to the outcome, and just enjoy each step for the experience of what it is.

(On pages 294–95 there is a chart, "20 Values," that you can use in the steps ahead.)

STEP I

Get your head around
the meaning of "values"

This step is designed to take a fairly abstract concept—values—and give it a human perspective and a personal frame of reference.

To begin, decide on a role model for yourself. This will not only be a person you admire *and* know well but someone who has been an influence on you at some stage of your life; for most of us, this rules out the Nelson Mandelas of the world.

Maybe this role model is your father or mother, or a relative, a work colleague, a teacher, or a spiritual guide. It's not really important who the person is, so much as what they're like—you need to know enough about them to be able to isolate their values.

Wait for a time when you're feeling calm and unpressured, with a spare half hour on your hands.

When you're relaxed, gently turn your thoughts to this role model. What are this person's qualities that most influence you? What do you most admire about them? Is it honesty? Assertiveness? A loving nature? Cheerfulness? Integrity? Determination? Irreverence?

If you can't put a word to these qualities but have a *feel* for what they mean to you, that's sufficient for the moment. The words will come later.

Think about this person before you move on to the next step.

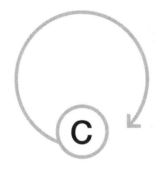

STEP 2
Take a peek
at the tables

Now that you've given some thought to certain values that others have—which you admire or have been influenced by—the next step is to make them more concrete. To do this, you may need to get a fix on what other values exist.

In the pages ahead you'll find a couple of tables designed to help broaden your view of these other possibilities. These lists are far from definitive, so feel free to add to them as you like. Use new words or phrases if that makes more sense to you.

The first is "A mini-list of life values." This is just a sample of qualities and attributes—words that may or may not mean anything to you. You can add to this list as you like. There's no limit to the values or qualities that could apply.

The second is "A mini-list of occupational values." As the name suggests, these words relate to the workplace, an area that dominates our lives in so many ways.

In both cases, only positive values have made it to the list, though I guess you could interpret some of them either way. Read through these, and make a casual note of any that strike a chord with you. (Use the "20 Values" chart on pages 294–95 to make a note of your thoughts. For the moment don't worry about the "1, 2, 3, 4" ranking columns.)

Don't analyze the individual words too much. Don't try to make them fit or follow any particular order. And, most important, don't try to rationalize why they might be appropriate or not; just go through the list and quickly note any that appeal. If none appeal, it doesn't matter in the slightest. They're designed to be thought-starters.

And whatever you do, take it easy—this is meant to be a relaxed look at yourself and what makes you tick, not an exhaustive, analytical exercise.

Simply choose 10–20 values you *feel* are important to your life right now, and jot them down. That's all. Be guided by your intuition.

A MINI-LIST OF LIFE VALUES

acceptance	achievement	acknowledgment	acquisition
adventure	affection	altruism	amazement
ambition	appreciation	approval	assertiveness
autonomy	balance	beauty	belonging
bliss	bravery	carefulness	caring
celebration	challenge	character	charity
charm	cheerfulness	commitment	compassion
competence	competition	confidence	conformity
connection	conservatism	consideration	contentment
control	cooperation	courage	creativity
credibility	curiosity	daring	decency
dedication	delight	dependability	detachment
determination	devotion	dignity	diligence
discipline	discrimination	duty	eccentricity
effectiveness	elegance	elitism	eloquence
empathy	empowerment	energy	enlightenment
enthusiasm	equality	excellence	excitement
exploring	fairness	faith	fame
family	fantasy	fidelity	flexibility
forgiveness	freedom	friendship	frugality
fulfillment	fun	generosity	gentleness
good health	goodness	grace	gratitude
growth	happiness	harmony	healing
helping	honesty	hope	humanity
humility	humor	idealism	inclusiveness
independence	individuality	industriousness	innocence
innovation	inspiration	integrity	intelligence
intimacy	intuition	irreverence	joy

kindness	knowledge	leadership	learning
leisure	liberalism	listening	logic
love	loyalty	mastery	maturity
meaning	mellowness	mercy	mindfulness
moderation	modesty	motivation	nobility
obedience	objectivity	open-mindedness	openness
optimism	order	pacifism	passion
patience	peace	perseverance	persistence
playfulness	politeness	positive	power
practicality	pragmatism	productivity	professionalism
prosperity	protest	prudence	purity
purpose	quality	rationality	realism
reason	recognition	reconciliation	reflection
relaxation	reliability	repentance	resignation
respect	responsibility	reverence	righteousness
sacrifice	sanity	satisfaction	security
self-confidence	self-control	self-esteem	self-respect
sensitivity	sensuality	sentimentality	serendipity
serenity	service	sharing	silence
simplicity	skepticism	smartness	sobriety
solidarity	spirituality	sportsmanship	stability
strength	success	superiority	support
surrender	tact	talent	taste
temperance	tenacity	tenderness	thankfulness
thoroughness	thrift	time	tolerance
triumph	trust	trustworthiness	truthfulness
understanding	unity	union	versatility
vision	vitality	wealth	well-being
wholesomeness	will	wisdom	wonder

A MINI-LIST OF OCCUPATIONAL VALUES

acquisition	ambition	appreciation	autonomy
balance	beauty	belonging	challenge
commitment	competence	confidence	conformity
control	cooperation	creativity	curiosity
dignity	effectiveness	excellence	excitement
fairness	family	friendship	good health
goodness	growth	harmony	honesty
humor	independence	individuality	intimacy
joy	kindness	knowledge	leadership
leisure	love	loyalty	meaning
modesty	peacefulness	pragmatism	prosperity
power	prudence	quality	respect
security	self-respect	sensitivity	serenity
sharing	simplicity	spirituality	stability
strength	success	trust	understanding
well-being	will	winning	wisdom

20 VALUES

	Value	1	2	3	4
1.					
2.					
3.					
4.					
5.					
6.					
7.					
8.					

	Value		1	2	3	4
9.						
10.						
11.						
12.						
13.						
14.						
15.						
16.						
17.						
18.						
19.						
20.						

STEP 3

Calmly refine your list

You've read through the two lists of values and jotted down a few words that struck a chord with you. There may be 10–20 words on your "20 Values" chart. A few more or less doesn't matter.

Now it's time to quickly evaluate your list—without thinking too much about each word—and whittle it down to something more manageable.

This should be fairly straightforward. Some of the words will fit neatly with what you suspect your core values are. But others may seem ambitious or even wildly romantic.

For example, if you're a timid and lazy person, it may not be realistic to keep the word "daring" on your values list—no matter how much it appeals—unless you're prepared to make the changes necessary to accomplish this. Better to focus on what you feel is important and possible in your life right now.

So, before we go any further, remove any unrealistic values from your list.

STEP 4

Play with the words

On your page are, say, 10 or so words that you *feel* may have some relevance to the way you live your life. Now it's time to bring these words to life. And, if necessary, to add to them.

To begin with, though, you need to flesh them out and turn them into your own language. I'll give you a couple of examples of how this could be done.

Let's say the word "peaceful" is on your list. You were attracted to the word, you thought it *felt* right, but you're not exactly sure that you could claim it as one of your core values.

However, you put the word on your list for a reason—even if the reason is not obvious to you. So let's explore a little to see if there are aspects of "peaceful" that are meaningful to you. Would it be more meaningful if you were to change it to "peace-loving"? Or "peace-making"? Or "seeking personal peace"? Any one of these extensions might produce the sentiment you've been looking for.

Or, say the word "competence" was on your list. While you might find it easy to understand the importance of being competent, and you might *feel* that such a quality could be important to your makeup, you're still not sure how it relates to you.

Let's take that word and play around with it, and see where it takes us:

$$competent = good\ at\ what\ you\ do$$
$$= striving\ to\ be\ better = doing\ your\ best$$

"Aha!" you say. "That's something I've been taught is imperative in life: no matter what you do, whether you win or lose, you must always do your best."

So, instead of having the word "competent" on your list, you now have something much more meaningful (to you): "doing your best."

If you're the only person who understands the relevance of this expression, that's fine. Because you're the only one who has to understand it! As long as it sums up what you feel, you've succeeded.

Once again, take it easy during this stage—treat it like a game.

STEP 5
Rank your values

Now it's time to put some shape into the words and phrases on your chart.

What we want to achieve here is a final list of four or five human values or qualities that you can confidently say give your life direction—in other words, you are going to identify your core values.

You may find you can rank them quite easily. If so, go ahead.

However, this ranking is not so obvious to most people. "Is honesty more important than generosity?" "Is loyalty more important than being satisfied with what you do?"

If you're in this "not-so-obvious" category, you'll find it easier to employ a couple more small steps to rank your categories.

The first step is to apply a simple formula.

Just mark each of the values on your list according to the following:

1 = very important
2 = somewhat important
3 = occasionally important
4 = not so important

If you had a relatively short list to start with, this may be all you need to do. But if you're still not sure, take it a step further.

Select only the values you've ranked 1 and 2. Divide each of these into one of the following categories (see the table below).

- "Essential"—these are central to the way you think and act at this very moment.
- "Important now"—these are slightly less important than the ones above.
- "Maybe later"—they're important but aren't necessarily on your horizon today. One day you'll work on them.

MY VALUES		
Essential	Important now	Maybe later

Ideally, you'll now have a list of five essential values. But if it feels right, there's no harm in having a few more or less. Whatever number you do arrive at, this is the list you'll be working with for some time to come. Make a note of these values below.

These are my main values:

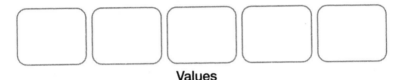

Values

When you're happy with the way these look, transfer them to the bottom row of "My influences chart" on page 352.

That's it.

If this process took a little longer than you thought, take comfort in the fact that you can use this list to help you work through many life issues, such as changing jobs, moving to another city, settling down with a potential life partner, or even less black-and-white issues such as personal ethics.

Better still, the steps are much easier from now on.

LEVEL 2: Your needs

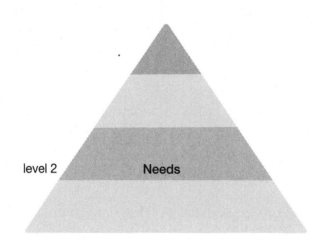

level 2   Needs

What are your needs?

Every human being has a set of basic human needs. While different academics might use different words to define these, their essence remains the same: on the one hand you have the needs that relate purely to your self-interest ("me"), and on the other you have the needs that refer to you and the role you play in the wider world. (See the table opposite.)

These are *basic* needs. They probably won't be the needs that are at the top of your mind right at this moment.

For example, if you own a comfortable home, the physical "need for shelter" might not seem relevant to you, even though it will certainly exist on an unconscious level. Conversely, if your family is threatened with eviction from your rented apartment, your need for shelter could be right at the top of the list.

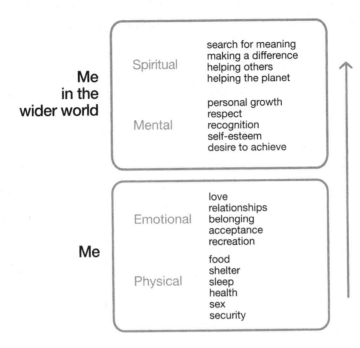

In practice, your more pressing needs will probably be the psychological—emotional, mental, and spiritual—issues of the day. Take a closer look at these and you'll discover a whole range of issues to focus your attention on. For example, if you feel you need a partner to make your life seem complete, "love" or "relationships" may be the need that tops your list. Or, if you've just come out of an abusive relationship, been fired from your job, and lost all your savings on an unsound investment, your need for "respect" or "tenderness" may seem much more important right now.

Your needs don't have to be defined in general terms such as those above. For example, I have a need to create and communicate—it would be difficult for me to conceive of a life where I could not exercise these abilities. So where I might write "the need to create" or "the need to communicate," someone else might write "the need for personal growth" or "the need to achieve."

All that matters is that the words mean something to you.

Even though your basic needs always exist, your most pressing needs will change from one year to the next—as you mature, as you make your way in the world, as relationships start and end, as you accomplish or fail in different ventures. This is why you need to revisit this part of the process from time to time.

For now, though, list below your five most pressing needs at this stage of your life.

Needs

When you're happy with the way they look, transfer them to the third row of "My influences chart" on page 352.

LEVEL 3: Your responsibilities

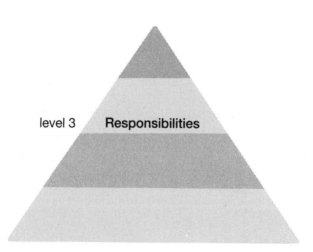

level 3   **Responsibilities**

Who's responsible?

Responsibilities. Obligations. What a burden they can be for some of us. Just look at the potential list!
- Family responsibilities and duties
- Work responsibilities
- Personal responsibilities
- Professional obligations
- Community responsibilities
- Moral or spiritual obligations

You might wonder where it all ends.

When you listed your values and your needs, you were dealing with personal influences—things that related only to you. Now we will introduce the external influences, where you're answerable, or believe you're answerable, to another. Sometimes many others.

Depending on the stage of life you're at, producing a list of your ongoing responsibilities will take very little effort.

Reducing that list to your five most prominent responsibilities or obligations will take a little more. But only a little.

When you trim down your list to the most important five, make a note of them here.

Responsibilities

When you're happy with the way they look, transfer them to the second row of "My influences chart" on page 352.

LEVEL 4: Your goals, ambitions, and desires

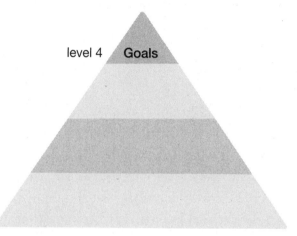

level 4 **Goals**

What drives you today?

The top level on our priorities pyramid is for your goals, ambitions, and desires. (The difference between the three is mostly your time frame: ambitions tend to be longer term, goals medium term, and desires more immediate.)

In an ideal world, these would be a natural development of what you've listed as your values, needs, and responsibilities.

If we choose two human values as examples—say, "reliability" and "leadership"—you'll see how these might logically flow on to your needs, your responsibilities, and your goals.

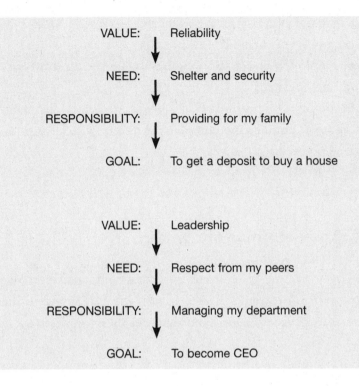

If you were dealing with something impersonal—such as a corporation—this neatness may be possible. But human beings tend to be more complex. Your goals or ambitions might not always connect back to a sound set of values. If you've always wanted to own a Ferrari, or you've dreamed for years about spending six months in Italy and you won't feel content until you've done so, then this may be an ambition that you should feature on your list. Maybe. Then, when you've achieved that particular goal, chances are you'll want to put something entirely different on your list.

Make a list of the things in life you really want for yourself—not things you have to think about but things that are in the forefront of your consciousness from one day to the next.

- Is it a material goal? Or an experience?
- Is it relationship-oriented? Or financial?
- Is it employment-related? Sports-related? Health-related? Community-related?
- Is it becoming a bit healthier? Or a major life accomplishment?
- Is it a project you need to complete? An exam you have to pass? A decision you must make?
- Is it a "must-have"? A possession?

Another way to rank your goals

If your goals are not as clear-cut as you would hope, and therefore more difficult to rank, there is a way you can approach them: simply rank them according to a time line. See the example on the next page.

In this example, your ultimate goal of being happy and content is made up of lots of smaller, more achievable goals along the way. Ultimately, the ones you would choose as your most important goals would relate to the time frame you had in mind: short term, medium term, or long term.

Whichever method you employ, it's important to edit your list down to the most important five. Then make a note of them here.

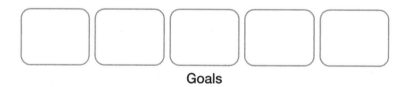

Goals

When you're happy with the way they look, transfer them to the top row of "My influences chart" on page 352.

Later

Happy &
content

Get
married

Appointed
CEO

Love   Satisfaction   Peer
respect

Join social
club

Get to know
directors

Dancing
lessons

Lose 15 lbs.

Management
course

Find calm
coach

Now

Adding it up

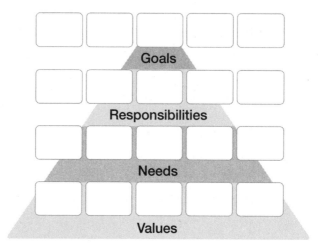

Your life on one page

If you've been updating the "My influences chart" on page 352, you'll now have a revealing document in front of you.

This is your life—your influences, your core values, your particular needs, your responsibilities, your goals and ambitions—neatly summarized.

When most people review their "My influences chart," they generally form one of three opinions.

- They think it looks like a stack of abstract words.
- They think it really sums up their drives and motivations.
- They say, "I already knew that."

Take another look at it and see which camp you fall into.

If you belong to the first—thinking it looks like a stack of abstract words—it's nothing to worry about. As long as you've taken the time to follow the steps to this point, the true power of what you have in front of you will soon be evident.

If you belong to the second group—thinking the chart really sums up your drives and motivations—so much the better.

If you belong to the third group, it may be that you know yourself exceptionally well, but it's more likely to be a case of emerging familiarity. After working your way through the discovery process, step by step on each of the levels, you may not be surprised when you finally see it all summarized like this. But if you think back a few days and try to imagine how you'd have responded if someone had asked about your core values and needs, you'll see how far you've come.

Your "My influences chart" now becomes the document you'll work with using the Life Priorities Calculator.

Later, as your needs, responsibilities, goals, and ambitions evolve— or as your focus becomes either shorter or longer in timing terms—you may choose to update it. But for the moment, this is your life.

So far you've completed the "groundwork"
phase of the Life Priorities Calculator.
- You have a clearer picture of what your core values are.
- You've worked out your most prominent needs.
- You've ranked your responsibilities and obligations.
- Your goals and ambitions are probably more
in alignment with the above.
Now it's time to use this information to define
and rank the priorities in your life.

The Life Priorities Calculator

PHASE 2

Welcome to the fun part

At the completion of this phase you'll have a list of the priorities
in your life—probably no more than four or five items—
and they will be ranked in order of importance.

Okay, the tedious bit is now out of the way. As is often the case
with groundwork, you spend a lot of time making it perfect and
then, at the end, all you have to show for your efforts is . . . well,
groundwork.

But as with all of life's endeavors, the better the preparation, the
easier it is to produce something great. And because we're concerned
with your life here—yes, your whole life—you'll probably see the
advantage in not cutting corners.

The formulation of your "My influences chart" was essentially left-brain in nature: structured, logical, and analytical. Now it's time to shift your attention to the fun phase.

You'll be pleased to note that this part is right-brain in nature: relaxed, intuitive, imaginative, and streamlined. It's fantasy time. There are no hard and fast rules here—other than to relax, enjoy, and let whatever happens happen.

Relax and let go

Why is it necessary to approach this second phase in a relaxed state of mind? Apart from the fact that it's more pleasant this way, it's also more effective, largely because of the way your brain works.

Some of the main influences in your life are unconscious. They direct you, inhibit you, shape your likes and dislikes, yet you're not even aware they're taking place, let alone understand why.

Paradoxically, the more you concentrate and try to work them out, the less apparent they become.

Generally, we all favor the rational, left hemisphere of our brain for thinking about issues like this. This allows a close-up, detailed perspective on what's going on. While this is okay for most of our daily activities, it's next to useless for being in touch with the "inner you" or understanding the big picture.

On the other hand, when you can *sense* what is going on around you, and you grasp important or big-picture scenarios, you are more than likely using a right-brain thinking style (intuitive, imaginative, holistic).

The way you feel plays a big role in determining which hemisphere of your brain you favor. When you feel edgy and tense, you automatically tend to favor a left-brain style of thinking—focused on detail, data, words, analysis, and logic. When you feel calm and relaxed, you automatically favor a right-brain style—imaginative, intuitive, and holistic.

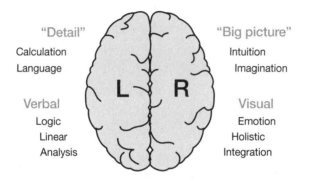

"Detail"   "Big picture"
Calculation   Intuition
Language   Imagination

Verbal   Visual
Logic   Emotion
Linear   Holistic
Analysis   Integration

The more relaxed you are, the more in tune you
are with your subconscious mind.

If you really relax now, yes relax, your thoughts will slow down. If you allow your imagination to drift free—maybe even taking you to another enjoyable place or experience altogether—your thought patterns will change. More peaceful. More sensual. More holistic.

Relax, and you are feeling more in tune with what's relevant to your life as a whole.

Relax, and you are more in touch with your intuition and instincts. The more you are relaxed, the better.

At the heart of your chart

You might think that because you've spent so much time developing your "My influences chart" it will be central to the final phase of the Life Priorities Calculator.

While it does play a role, it's not a central one. Sorry. The chart was a means of helping you sort through your values, needs, responsibilities, and goals; if you have completed it, you will have sorted through these issues to the best of your abilities. Now, before you move on to the next step, all you have to do is give the previous steps a brief once-over.

Take a couple of minutes now to reflect on the content before you. And however you choose to reflect, take it easy. You don't have to memorize any details—just look them over and, if it's meant to happen, absorb their meaning.

> "My influences chart" is a tool for your subconscious.
> There's no need for you to analyze it or even understand it.

Some time in the future

Treat the following four exercises as alternatives—choose one that takes your fancy or try them all. All that matters is that you settle on one that feels right to you at this particular time.

Each exercise uses a resource you've been perfecting since childhood: the ability to pretend, to use your imagination, to escape the "here and now," and to go to some place in the distant, or not-so-distant, future.

Why turn to your imagination rather than your intellect?

One of the most common frames of mind we encounter in the workplace is one that rejects intuition and gut feeling and will respond only to what we believe are hard facts and data: the things we can assess with our senses, the things we can see, hear, and read about.

This is an understandable response from people who are locked into left-brain-style thinking patterns and activities, as is often the case during a normal workday.

Unfortunately, this kind of thinking is limited by its narrow focus. If you really want to grasp a big concept—such as what makes you who you are—you need to employ *all* your mental potential. The way to do this is to step away from this fixation with hard facts and data and to start using the right side of your brain as well as the left.

Each of the following exercises is designed to shift you from your comfortable left-brain world of facts and logic into the exciting right-brain realm of fantasy, feelings, and imagination. Here you are less restricted by the narrowness of your everyday needs and responsibilities and are more able to tap into the feelings and motivations that shape your life but may not be immediately apparent to you.

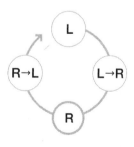

You start in a focused left-brain frame of mind.

Now, relaxing and using your imagination, you allow your thinking to become more right-brain in style—until you are totally relaxed and relying on your intuition.

Then you return to your focused left-brain state to review what you've achieved.

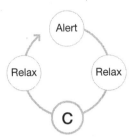

Or it may seem easier if you look at it another way.

Imagine the whole process as a fluid, circular activity—one in which you gradually move from an alert, concentrating frame of mind to one that's completely relaxed and calm (C). Then you work your way back.

So, you'd move from:

- an alert left-brain state where you analyze, evaluate, review
- to a progressively more relaxed state where you begin to occupy your mind with anything but the issue at hand
- to a calm, right-brain state where you forget all that's going on and maybe get lost in your imagination or some distracting activity
- back to a slightly more focused state where you make note of your feelings and impressions
- all the way back to the alert left-brain state that you started from, where you analyze and evaluate your conclusions.

To put all of the above into practice, all you have to do is follow these five steps:

1. Review "My influences chart" for 60 seconds.
2. Allow yourself to unwind.
3. Go to an imaginary place.
4. Accept every answer.
5. Evaluate later.

Make a note of these steps, because they are central to most of the exercises in the pages ahead.

1. Review for 60 seconds

Very briefly, cast an eye over your "My influences chart" (page 352). Without articulating any of the words or trying to remember them in any way, let them sink in for 60 seconds or so.

Then put the chart away somewhere. This is the last time you'll refer to it.

2. Allow yourself to unwind

As I mentioned before, these exercises are designed to be performed in as relaxed a state as you can manage. So the first step is to put aside a half hour—or more if you need the time to really unwind—and just take it easy.

Go and sit under a big, beautiful tree. Or run a warm bath. Or just recline in a comfortable chair. Have a large pad and pencil beside you as you relax there.

You have no agenda here. There is nothing much you have to prepare for or think about. Just allow yourself the luxury of slowing down, relaxing, and letting go.

3. Go to an imaginary place

This is the incubation part: a time of indulgence and fantasy, with no objective other than to have a good time and relax.

If you're one of those who say, "I have no imagination," it's okay. The exercises that follow take this into account.

In this imaginary place, there is nothing you have to think about, or work on, or achieve. It's just a relaxing, pleasurable time of escape. Enjoy it.

When you're feeling relaxed, with nothing much on your mind, let your thoughts wander to the things that are important to you. (The exercises that follow will make this easy.)

Maybe these are things you've been too busy to think about for years but were once very important to you. Maybe they're things you've neglected because your focus has been on other more pressing activities. Maybe they're qualities you've admired in others and have been meaning to cultivate in yourself.

Without being too structured about this, consider the following questions.

- What do you value most in life?
- What gives your days meaning?
- What gives your work meaning?
- What aspects of your life or work make you feel proud?
- What gives you great joy? And satisfaction?
- What qualities or values do you admire in other people that you hope other people might see in you?
- If you had all the time in the world, which of your human qualities would you like to develop and perfect?

Or if you'd like to be a little more structured in your thoughts, try using a "decision list" as a prompt. Put together a list, something like the following, then rate the various items in order of importance to you.

- I was a success in my job.
- I earned a lot of money from my work.
- I rose to the top of my profession.
- I helped others and shared my good fortune with them.

- I became managing director.
- I owned a fabulous house and car.
- I worked at my relationships with friends.
- I spent my best moments with my family.
- I took the time to develop my relationship with my partner.
- I taught others how to maximize their skills.
- I had some fantastic vacations.
- I learned many life-enriching skills not related to my work.
- I found every day to be an adventure.
- I wrote a book/built a house/learned the violin/sailed around the world/earned a PhD.
- I took good care of my health.
- I spent every moment I could with my children when they were young.

Now, just take it easy and allow yourself to relax even more.

4. Accept every answer

Have you ever noticed that when you're really relaxed and laid-back, with nothing on your mind, your mind brims with good ideas? They seem to come from all directions.

This phenomenon is a natural part of being in a relaxed right-brain frame of mind. We're going to use this unique ability to bring your subconscious thoughts into focus.

The key to making them useful is to avoid trying to evaluate them when they arise. This takes a little discipline—especially when you think you have a good idea. But it is essential.

Jot down anything that springs to mind—partial ideas, complete ideas, words, pictures, phrases, anything. The words you use may not make a lot of sense but write them down nevertheless. Maybe you'll find it easier to produce simple doodles or drawings instead. Just put them down and don't spare them another thought at this stage.

The object is not to edit or to dismiss anything that comes to mind, just to make a record of it so you can evaluate later.

If you believe you're the type who can't resist editing and analyzing as you go along, try this simple exercise: We call it "Yes . . . And."

Say an outrageous thought comes to mind. "I'm wearing a Spiderman suit." Instead of assessing this, wondering what it means or rejecting it outright, you simply apply this formula: "Yes, I'm wearing a Spiderman suit. And . . ." and then move to the next thought. In this way, you are continually moving forward and remain open to new ideas.

5. Evaluate later

You've been through the indulgent phase. You relaxed, distracted yourself with a fantasy or two, and jotted down any thoughts that came to mind.

Now it's time to evaluate them. You can do this at any time you like.

This is a straightforward process—one that you'll probably find the most logical. It's a businesslike left-brain procedure. You take each of the notes you've made on your page and ask, "What does this mean? What was my subconscious trying to tell me?"

Often, you'll have all the answers you need right there in front of you. The task is complete.

Sometimes, though, some of the words or expressions that come to mind may seem obscure or even meaningless. Maybe they are. Yet there is always the possibility that they contained clues about important feelings and motivations that exist on a subconscious level.

If this is so, the challenge is to explore these clues to see where they lead. This is something you can do now or at a later stage.

The five steps

So there you have the five steps common to all the exercises in the pages ahead.

1. Review "My influences chart" for 60 seconds.
2. Allow yourself to unwind.
3. Go to an imaginary place.
4. Accept every answer.
5. Evaluate later.

Take your pick of the following exercises and let's see how the above five steps apply.

Choose an exercise

The exercises that follow take place in your imagination.
If you believe you're one of those types who has no imagination,
or who finds it difficult to visualize, don't give it another thought.
All you have to do to succeed is *pretend* to play out the role.
It doesn't matter how superficial your pretense, it will have
the desired effect on your subconscious.

There are four different exercises for you to choose from. You'll only need one to achieve what you want to achieve, but feel free to use more if the fancy takes you.

Each exercise is slightly different in its intent and its effect. So each will have a different appeal to different personality types.

The exercises are designed to polarize—so if one appeals to you yet seems alien or silly to someone else, this is exactly how it's meant to be. Just be guided by what feels right, and you'll choose the right one.

Each exercise is designed to do two things.

- Help you explore further than what you currently "know" about yourself—that is, to make you more receptive to your subconscious as well as your conscious understandings.
- Play down the very real (though not always obvious) influences of your ego.

Depending on your particular needs and personality, the subconscious part may be more important than the ego part, or vice versa. Be guided by what *feels* right—even on the most superficial level.

End of days

Set aside half an hour for the following exercise. After you have reviewed your "My influences chart," go somewhere quiet and private where you won't be disturbed. Outdoors, in a patch of warm sun would be ideal, but anywhere will do. Take a blanket and a large pad and a pencil.

The idea is to imagine yourself as an elderly person, nearing the end of your days on earth and reviewing the kind of things that might go through your mind at that time of life. Take care not to make this forlorn or pitiful, but consider it as a positive time where you are happy, content, and satisfied with having accomplished most of what you set out to accomplish in life.

To stimulate your subconscious, you can flesh out the role a bit: pull the blanket over your lap; hold one wrinkled hand in another; and tell yourself there's nothing you have to do but just sit back and enjoy the sunshine.

Allow yourself a few minutes to relax and get used to the luxury of having lots of extra time on your hands.

Close your eyes. Let your imagination drift. Try to feel what it's like to actually be in this role . . . at whatever age you're imagining . . . where you live entirely for the moment . . . with no future pressures on your agenda . . . content just to sit there and relax . . . looking back over the life you've led.

Looking back. Looking back. Reviewing what made you happy, satisfied, and fulfilled.

Which features of the years you've spent do you consider most important? Was it your career achievements? The wealth you amassed? The relationships you had and still have? Was it that you spent your best moments with your children, or fostering your relationships? Was it that you achieved the best you were capable of in every undertaking? Was it that you helped others? Was it that you made a difference to the world at large, to your community, or to your family and friends? What's most important to you now?

Whatever thoughts come to mind, make a note of them. Every one. You will review these later.

Remote viewing

Set aside half an hour for this exercise. Review your "My influences chart," then go somewhere quiet and private where you won't be disturbed. Take a large pad and a pencil. The place you go to could reflect the type of scenario you're going to immerse yourself in—near the water, in open spaces, in the cool shade of a tree.

The objective of this exercise is to imagine yourself in a place where there are no worldly distractions—a place with no deadlines, no obligations, and no one around to criticize or be impressed. For example . . .

- It could be on a sailboat out in the wide, featureless ocean. Several days from land, perfect weather, and no schedule or destination in mind.

- It could be in the middle of a vast expanse of land: the Arctic, the Sahara, the Australian outback, the Grand Canyon. No one for miles. Absolute stillness. Perfect weather.

- It could be on a mountaintop. Warm sun and gentle breeze on your face. The 360-degree horizon stretching out before you.

- It could be on a secluded beach on a tropical island. Gleaming sands. Abundant fruit. The soft lapping of waves.

Look into the distance and let your eyes go out of focus. Relax. Let your tensions go. Whatever this imaginary place is, you feel at home here. You are comfortable, secure, with all your needs taken care of.

When you can imagine yourself in this place—remote from all the pressures and distractions of everyday life, detached from what the world thinks of you and how you like to present yourself to it—gently turn your thoughts to yourself. The *essential* you.

What are the things, experiences, possessions, and people that make you feel happy, content, fulfilled? What aspects of life do you now consider most important? Is it career achievements? Is it the size of your house or the make of car you drive? Is it the relationships you have? Is it your family? Is it that you are a trusted and respected member of your community? Is it that you achieved the best you were capable of—whatever you undertook? Is it that you helped others? Is it that you made a difference?

What's been important to you in the past? What's most important to you now?

Whatever thoughts come to mind, make a note of them. Review these in a while.

The wake test

(This exercise is not for the emotionally fragile. If you're feeling unhappy or you've been ill, perhaps you should pass over this one and try one of the others.)

Set aside half an hour for this exercise. Review your "My influences chart," then go somewhere quiet where you won't be disturbed, preferably indoors. Take a large pad and a pencil.

The key to this exercise is to approach it with humor. Make it light-hearted, almost tongue-in-cheek. Why? Because you're going to be attending your own wake. Don't worry—it's only in your imagination.

As you close your eyes and relax, allowing your mind to clear, stepping aside from the mundane events of your everyday life, enjoying the fact that you have a whole half hour with nothing to do but fantasize, turn your thoughts to this event.

Imagine you're standing at the door, or looking through the window, or floating above the gathering, and nobody can see you.

Cheer up. It's not one of those glum, morbid affairs. This is a fun event held in your honor. And it's all the more fun for you because you can be there to witness it all.

Everyone you've ever known, loved, or respected has turned up. They're not here to mourn but to celebrate your life—what you were (are), what you meant to them, what you achieved, what they learned from you.

Each attendee is allowed a few minutes to tell the gathering about your qualities, about what made you unique.

What are they saying? Are they talking about how you forced your way up the corporate ladder? Or how you invested wisely? Or how good a golfer, bridge player, or raconteur you were? Or are they praising your qualities as a friend, leader, lover, or parent?

Whatever thoughts their words stimulate, write them down. Review these later.

The naked truth

This exercise isn't for everyone, so read through and see if it's right for you. Although it is meant to make you feel uncomfortable, it's not meant to turn you off. And it won't work if you're an exhibitionist.

(In case you're wondering, this exercise has never been performed at one of our training programs.)

Set aside half an hour for the exercise. Review your "My influences chart," then go somewhere quiet, warm, and very private. Take a large pad and a pencil.

Now strip.

Yes, take off all your clothes. The lot. If you feel silly and exposed sitting there naked—*good*. That is the intention. The purpose of this exercise is to disengage from ego, pretense, and worldly accomplishment, and come face to face with the real you.

Now, allow yourself to relax and "acclimatize" for a few minutes.

When you feel calm and relaxed, close your eyes and tell yourself that just for the moment you are detached from your earthly trappings—appearance, status, accomplishments, habits, and needs. Tell yourself that all these things are just a costume, and the *real* you is something deeper and more essential. The *essential* you considers some things important and others not, even though they may be the most pressing issues in your daily life. The missed promotion, the poor investment, the ongoing tension with your colleague—at this moment, such things may not seem all that important in the grand scheme of your life.

So, what is important?

Whatever thoughts come to mind, make a note of them. Then you can review what you've written later.

What do you do now?

Now that you've acted out the role or enjoyed the imaginary scenario, what have you achieved?

On the most basic level, a half hour with one of those exercises should be relaxing and enjoyable in its own right. So, if nothing else, you should be feeling a little more content and at ease than when you started.

There is a slight chance that by now you will have a complete list of your life priorities: five or six items, in order, which you can use as a road map for making your way through life.

It is more likely, though, that you won't have such a black-and-white outcome. Yet.

Generally, these imaginary exercises will produce one of the following reactions in you:

- Wow, I've discovered things about myself, and what's important to me, that I never suspected were the case.
- Although I'd never really put this into words, I'm not particularly surprised about what I've learned.
- I knew all that. (True, I had forgotten about it as I matured.)
- I've got a bunch of words on a pad that I've no idea what to do with.
- Oops. I forgot to write the words altogether. I'll write them down now.

Each of those responses is normal. Each is appropriate, depending on your experience and the type of person you are. And each of them leads naturally to the conclusion of this exercise.

Now it's a simple step to take it to the next stage: a short list of the priorities in your life.

Probably, this list will *not* be what you have on the pad in front of you. What you have there refers to thoughts and sentiments you brought to the surface. At this moment these words are just a stimulus, a reminder, a subconscious clue, of an experience that took place only in your imagination.

Now, without thinking too hard, without analyzing too much, write down the most relevant priorities in your life. Straight off the top of your head. What are the main priorities in your life?

Write them on the table on the next page. Five to seven items.

PRIORITIES

Priority	1	2	3	4
1.				
2.				
3.				
4.				
5.				
6.				
7.				

Once you've written them down, give them a rating: 1 is essential; 4 is not quite so essential.

Don't think about this too much, just do it as quickly and fluidly as you can.

The four, five, or even six items on your list that you've given the highest ratings (that is, the lowest number) are the priorities of your life—in order. Write them down in the table below—in order.

Priorities

1

2

3

4

5

6

When you are happy with this list, transfer it to the "My priorities chart" on page 353. On that same chart you'll also find space to include your values, needs, responsibilities, and goals, so that you have all your life influences on the one page.

This becomes an important reference point that you can use from now on.

What if you can't decide?

Often, when you have two priorities that are important to you, it will seem difficult to discard one in favor of the other.

When this situation occurs, you can add more resources to your decision-making process.

Say you're trying to determine whether A is more important to you than B, or vice versa. Try this simple test.

- Hold your arms out in front of you. Relax and close your eyes.
- Imagine you are "holding" one of the items in each hand. On your left is A ("making sure my children have the best education"). On your right is B ("moving closer to the schools").
- Now, which one *feels* heavier?

That's all you have to do. The heavier one is the one you want; it's your intuition's way of guiding you to the right choice for you. This little test is a good way of moving away from all the information and logic and using your subconscious to help you make the decision. Later, if it doesn't feel right to you, change it.

Your list

There they are. Your life priorities. Were they as you expected when you first opened this book?

Among the many lists I've seen people produce, there have been frequent references to making a difference, to developing and nurturing good relationships with friends and loved ones, to developing life-enriching skills, to writing cookbooks, to creating healthy and happy opportunities for children, to getting the utmost satisfaction from each day.

Perhaps not surprisingly, there have been very few lists that mentioned career positions, real estate portfolios, or brand of car.

This is not to suggest that one person's priority is superior to another's. Every person is different. Your priorities will almost certainly be different from the next person's. All that matters is that they're yours; you know what they are and you believe in them.

The final test

Say, for example, the list of priorities you've created was like the one on the next page.

On the surface, there's nothing surprising here. You feel comfortable with your list. But this is an important list; how can you be sure that, deep down, these are the priorities that are most relevant to you?

On an intellectual level, you'll probably have no difficulty assessing them and determining their appropriateness. But what about at a deeper level? What does your subconscious say about this?

We've devised a simple test to help you take these words and see how your subconscious responds to them. It all happens in

Priorities

> 1 *Ensuring that all the members of my family are happy, healthy, and prosperous*

> 2 *Having a secure job that allows me time to spend with my family*

> 3 *Remaining fit and healthy through daily exercise*

> 4 *Being debt-free*

> 5 *Sharing some of my good fortune with those less fortunate*

your imagination. And the best time to do it is when you're feeling relaxed and carefree.

If it takes half an hour to ease yourself into this state, it will be half an hour well spent.

Start now

When you are feeling comfortable and relaxed, it's time to start the pretense. You're going for a job interview. You have no idea what the job is, what the duties are, or what the pay and conditions are. All you have to guide you is a description of the person they are seeking. Your imaginary interviewer explains that the person they are looking for is someone who shares your list of priorities.

Using the priorities listed above, your imaginary interviewer would say: "The person we are looking for . . . is primarily focused on ensuring that her family is happy, healthy, and prosperous. She is attracted to this job because it's secure and allows plenty of family time. The person we're looking for will be fit and healthy and will probably be debt-free. And, finally, she will believe it's important to share her good fortune with those less fortunate."

Now, there is one question to ask yourself: Is this the job for you? Even without knowing the details of the position, do you feel that you are the right person for it?

If you answer yes, then your list of life priorities fits comfortably with how you see yourself on a deeper level. If you answer no, then you probably need to revisit some of the earlier steps.

Staying flexible

Your priorities—for now

Now that you've gone through all these steps and defined your life priorities, you might think the last thing you want to read is that these could change. But as your life changes, so do your needs and responsibilities. And your priorities. Even your values may change sometimes.

So no matter how orderly you think your life is at this moment, no matter how much effort you've invested in working through your values and priorities, things never quite continue the way you plan.

If you lose your job, or get evicted from your apartment, or meet the most fantastic person who's ever walked this earth (and who wants to take you to live on the other side of the globe), the direction of your life is probably going to change. When that happens, your priorities tend to change as well.

So, too, when you enter different phases of life—when you

change jobs or partners, when you have children, when you go to funerals, when unforeseen events occur, when your state of health alters, as you discover new passions, as you grow older.

All changes represent a great opportunity to take another look at your life and, if need be, to re-prioritize.

Now, however, this is much easier to do because you have a way—a *calm* way—of bringing your priorities into focus whenever you feel the need.

This is your list. No one else ever has to see or know about it. You can add to it, reshape it, redo it to your heart's content. Moreover, you *should* redo it from time to time to ensure that your life is on track.

Your priorities—for the rest of your life

The beauty of having completed the Life Priorities Calculator is that you will soon be able to sidestep many of the stresses and pressures of your daily life and learn how to keep events in perspective. It will give you the ability to concentrate on the activities that will serve you best and to make decisions with much more confidence than has been possible in the past.

And, perhaps most important of all, once you have your priorities in perspective, you'll be more able to restore balance to the many competing aspects of your day.

While the benefits of being able to do this may be incremental, they add up to a massive improvement in all aspects of your life— from the way you feel, to your state of health, to what you are able to aspire to and achieve.

Use the calculator now. Use it whenever change comes along. Use it whenever you want to change or enhance your focus in life.

And, above all, use it for the sheer enjoyment of being able to take some time out of your busy schedule, so you can relax and discover there's much more to YOU than you might otherwise have thought.

Quite a good result for knowing what your priorities are, don't you think?

Finding purpose

Turning priorities into purpose

For the purposes of this book, you will have achieved everything you set out to achieve once you've developed your list of priorities. This following step is a bonus that you can use now or at any time in the future.

You probably weren't expecting this book to go further than its original promise of helping you determine your life's priorities. However, I felt it would be a pity to come so far in the process of self-discovery, then not take the final step—exploring what your life's *purpose* is.

Priorities and purpose are two different things. Yet even when they're unrelated, they can still be the products of the same process.

Purpose relates not to what you do or who you live with but to the issue of your life itself. The role of your purpose is to guide and inspire. When it is clearly defined, it provides direction for all your actions and decisions, both immediate and long term. The clearer your purpose, the better off you'll be.

So if you want to lead a happy, balanced, and successful life, you need to approach it with purpose—with a clear idea of your values and priorities. Approaching it with a strong sense of purpose is the surest way to:

- feel in control of your life
- ensure that what you do each day—work, play, relationships, decisions—dovetails with your more fundamental needs and drives
- maximize your skills and talents and function at full capacity without having to question or review each step
- get maximum joy and satisfaction from what you do
- be able to relax and go with life's flow.

Purpose puts you in control

In an earlier chapter we touched on the basic needs that *all* human beings have to satisfy to one degree or another. At the top of this list of needs is the search for meaning: What am I here for? What is my life about?

Whether or not you categorize this as a spiritual need, such questions will cross your mind at some time or another—most frequently at times of crisis or dejection, though sometimes at happier times.

For most of us, though, it's not something we think much about. We're usually too busy, preoccupied, or locked into routine to be so introspective. We think we've achieved a lot just getting through the day, let alone pausing to ask why we've done it or what it all means.

But sooner or later you will ask these questions. What gives my life direction? How can I make the most of what I am? Why am I here?

A strong sense of purpose is the most fundamental definition of what drives you. Ideally, it should go deeper than the external influences on your life such as family, friends, citizenship, career, and religion. When it does, you will feel you are in full control of your life.

Some people believe that having goals or ambitions is the same as having a strong sense of purpose. It's not. Goals and ambitions are short-term and limited and serve a vastly different need than your life's purpose.

I'll give you an example. Say we have a psychologist who is determined to become the most influential academic in his field. Is this a goal or a purpose?

Use this simple test: Does it apply to all of his life or just one aspect of it?

Obviously, becoming "the most influential academic" applies to just one aspect, so you'd have to say it was a goal. The difference would become very clear to the psychologist if he was suddenly fired from his post, with a tarnished reputation that made further employment in his field unlikely—he'd feel that he had lost control over his life.

Let's take another approach. Say this same psychologist's purpose was "to spread peace and calm to all he comes in contact with."

If he were to lose his position now, how would he react? Sure, he'd still be unhappy, but he would feel some measure of control over the direction of his life because he could still follow his purpose of spreading peace and calm—perhaps even in another field.

Keeping it in perspective

Because so many benefits flow from having a strong sense of purpose, you might come to the conclusion that it should be something splendid like saving the planet, curing cancer, or transforming humankind.

Nothing could be further from the truth.

Many definitions of a life purpose will seem relatively mundane—healing or teaching, for example—yet these can make the greatest contribution to society and can be the most motivating and fulfilling to follow.

We're searching for a single statement that would immediately communicate to anyone what your life is about.

What are the guidelines for developing your sense of purpose?

- First and foremost, it will be positive (so it's about feeling or doing rather than stopping or preventing).
- It will extend you and make you want to move toward something, though it doesn't necessarily have to involve any action.
- It will be focused on something larger, perhaps more "important," than just yourself. Yet it will not necessarily be noble or about giving or goodness.
- It will have the potential to become a passion that you live (or maybe even die) for, something you will dedicate your life to.
- It will align with all of your values and will accommodate your lifelong dreams, concerns, and ambitions.
- It will have a deeper reason behind it, so that it's more than just something you might do; it's something you stand for and believe in as well.

What does a purpose look like?

There is *nothing* more personal in life than your life purpose. However, so that you can get this concept of "my purpose" into perspective, it will help if you have some idea how other people have expressed theirs. As you read through these, you'll note that not one of them refers to money, possessions, or position. And each is quite different from a goal or an ambition.

My purpose is to spread peace, calm, and happiness though my abilities as a communicator.

My purpose is to help small children discover ways of expressing themselves through music and art.

My purpose is to create an environment that encourages my children and grandchildren to be the best they can be.

My purpose is to nurture and show love through cooking and good health.

My purpose is to teach others the important lessons from history.

My purpose is to help older people overcome loneliness and enjoy some of the benefits of family life.

My purpose is to spread love and find the appealing side of everyone I come in contact with.

My purpose is to serve my god by helping others in any way I can.

My purpose is to heal and alleviate suffering.

My purpose is to restore and preserve some of the quality of life on our planet for future generations.

My purpose is to help people rise above the limitations of poverty.

Some of these examples are modest, while others are grand. Some are generic, while others are specific. They are not in any way meant to be ideals. They're just what some individuals thought was important to them. What works for others is irrelevant; all that's important is what works for you.

How to determine your life's purpose

When we talk about your life's purpose, we're talking about something profound and potentially life-changing. In its most basic sense, it's a road map for the rest of your life. Ideally, it is a mission so compelling that it draws you toward it.

With something so vital to your well-being, it's probably too much to expect a clear-cut answer to immediately spring to mind.

Finding the perfect description of your life's purpose usually takes time. Some people hit on it right away, while others nip and tuck until it feels absolutely right.

Whether it takes a day or a year, there's a hard way to approach this and there's the Calm Way.

The hard way involves ongoing struggle and analysis. Then, if all goes according to plan, on some distant day in the future you may become enlightened in some way or another.

The Calm Way is simply to create the environment in which the appropriate answer arrives of its own accord. And if it turns out that this is not the answer you're looking for, you simply have another go at it. What could be easier than that?

The steps

Unlike what was done with the other segments of this book, I'm not going to give you a simple formula that will define your life's purpose in four easy steps. However, I am going to give you the four easy steps that will *help* you work out your life's purpose. The result may not be instant and it may not even be what you'd call fast, but it will eventually produce the answer you're looking for.

1. Get in touch with yourself

As you are well aware, you are most in tune with your "real" self when you're deeply relaxed, alone, and in absolute quiet. But there are other occasions when you get in touch to this level. Sometimes you'll be moved by an event—real or dramatized, such as in a movie or play. Maybe you'll get deeply involved in a discussion or debate over an issue that you seem to care about more than others. Other times you'll find yourself deeply engrossed in some activity to the exclusion of everything else.

At these times, you'll get a *feel* for some issue or other that affects you deeply. Make a note of this.

2. Ask questions

"What am I all about?" Make a list of the qualities or passions or talents—even those you seldom notice or think about—that make you who you are.

"What do I feel strongly about?" Make a list of these as well.

3. Reflect

Go somewhere quiet and allow yourself to relax and slow down. Let your mind drift back over your life and make a note of any events, experiences, achievements, or even thoughts that you found to be particularly moving, fulfilling, or meaningful. When did you feel most powerful and effective? When did you feel that everything "just fell into place"?

Make a list of these things. Particularly note anything they have in common.

4. Review

Perform this step on a different occasion from the first three (but after you have performed 1, 2, and 3). Once again, go somewhere quiet and allow yourself to relax and slow down.

Taking all the information from the previous three steps—the qualities or characteristics that make you "you," the things you feel deeply about, the past experiences that were most meaningful to you—consider what they all add up to.

What phrase most sums up the important motivations in your life? If something compelling comes to mind, make a note of it.

Later, when you review this note, if you don't feel completely at home with its sentiment, if it doesn't encourage you to move ahead and put it into practice, each of these above steps probably needs to be revisited. If this happens, it's okay. Sometimes your purpose takes a while to surface. But it *is* there somewhere. And it *is* waiting to surface. When the time is right, it will happen.

As long as you keep an open mind and are receptive to an answer, one will come.

And when it does, you will recognize it by the fact that it motivates you, makes you feel fulfilled (even before you put it into play), and maybe even scares you a little.

Now, what do you do with it?

When you finally do arrive at a suitable articulation of your life's purpose, what are you going to do with it?

To put it into play, to use it to shape your life and give it direction, you do require a degree of commitment.

But once you've committed yourself to it, your purpose becomes a driving force in its own right. It becomes your measure for what's right and wrong. It becomes the framework for your big decisions. It becomes your motivation to grow and succeed. And, most rewarding of all, the more you use it, the more fulfilling your life becomes.

A clear path ahead

Now that you've worked out your priorities—and perhaps defined your purpose—you can approach life with more confidence and clarity. You can focus on getting what you most want, rather than being distracted or losing sleep over issues that might not be so important to you.

Consider the following example.

- If you placed "becoming the most influential lawmaker in the country" at the top of your priorities list, you now know exactly where to apply your efforts. Then, the fact that you might have to forego some of your family time in order to accomplish this would become an acceptable sacrifice.

- If you placed "more quality time with my family" at the top of your list, you'd know exactly where your priorities lay in relation to your job. It doesn't mean you'd ignore your work responsibilities, but it does mean you'd be able to endure being passed over for promotion.

Each of us has only a certain amount of psychic and physical energy to devote to our life activities. To spread that energy too thin or to waste it on activities that are unimportant to us leads to strain and inefficiency. To focus on only one thing at a time is not only more peaceful and orderly but more efficient.

When you focus on the activities that are most important to you now, you'll discover that not only do the stresses and frustrations of daily life begin to fade, but you will also get more joy and satisfaction from what you do.

Peace, joy, and satisfaction? Can you think of any better reward for knowing what's important in life?

Your tools

My influences chart

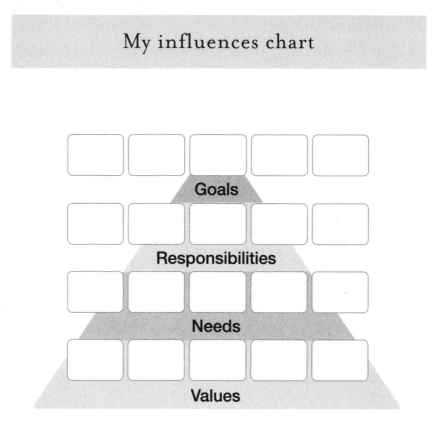

My priorities chart

Priorities

1

2

3

4

5

6

A MINI-LIST OF LIFE VALUES

acceptance	creativity	freedom	moderation
achievement	credibility	friendship	modesty
adventure	curiosity	fulfillment	motivation
affection	daring	fun	objectivity
ambition	decency	generosity	openness
appreciation	dedication	goodness	optimism
approval	delight	gratitude	passion
assertiveness	dependability	happiness	patience
autonomy	detachment	honesty	perseverance
balance	determination	hope	persistence
beauty	devotion	humanity	playfulness
belonging	dignity	humility	politeness
bravery	diligence	humor	pragmatism
caring	discipline	idealism	professionalism
celebration	duty	independence	prosperity
challenge	eccentricity	individuality	purpose
charity	effectiveness	innocence	quality
charm	eloquence	innovation	rationality
cheerfulness	empathy	inspiration	realism
commitment	energy	integrity	reason
compassion	enlightenment	intelligence	recognition
competence	enthusiasm	intimacy	relaxation
confidence	equality	irreverence	reliability
connection	excellence	joy	respect
consideration	excitement	kindness	responsibility
contentment	fairness	leadership	satisfaction
control	family	logic	security
cooperation	flexibility	love	self-confidence
courage	forgiveness	maturity	

self-control	solidarity	talent	trustworthiness
self-respect	spirituality	taste	truthfulness
sensitivity	sportsmanship	tenacity	understanding
sentimentality	stability	tenderness	union
serenity	strength	thankfulness	versatility
sharing	success	thoroughness	vision
simplicity	support	thrift	wealth
skepticism	surrender	time	wisdom
sobriety	tact	tolerance	

Work out the priorities
for your organization

If you'd like to determine your priorities or bring Perfect Balance
to yourself, your business, or your organization—on a much larger
scale than is possible from a book—discover how to do it at this web
address:

www.thecalmway.com

There is probably no more appropriate person to conceive of *Perfect Balance* than Paul Wilson.

He thrives in a number of worlds where peace and life balance are longed for but seldom achieved. As well as being an international bestselling author, he is a father, businessman, business strategic consultant, music producer, meditation teacher, and director of a medical research foundation.

Paul is known as the "guru of calm." He has created a string of bestsellers on the topic of calm—ranging from his introduction to meditation, *The Calm Technique*, to *Instant Calm* and *Calm at Work*, to the inspired *Little Book of Calm*—which have been translated into dozens of languages.

For almost thirty years he has been developing and refining a unique approach to finding contentment and performing well in high-pressure environments. The Calm Way™ works on the principle that the best way to accomplish your goals is not by trying to work harder—which is often likely to be counterproductive—but by adopting a more relaxed and balanced approach.